the radical bible

adapted by
John Eagleson
and
Philip Scharper
from
bibel provokativ
edited by
Hellmut Haug
and
Jurgen Rump
translated by
Erika J. Papp

ORBIS BOOKS
Maryknoll, New York
1972

Originally published as *bibel provokativ*.
© 1969 by Württembergische Bibelanstalt Stuttgart
Verlag Katholisches Bibelwerk GmbH Stuttgart

Copyright © 1972, ORBIS BOOKS
Maryknoll, N.Y. 10545
Library of Congress
Catalog Card Number: 76-190164

Manufactured in the
United States of America.

table of contents

introduction

rad´ i· cal (răd i· kăl, adj. [l l radicalis having roots, fr. radix -icis, a root.] 1. Of, pert. to, or proceeding from the root. 2. Original; fundamental; reaching to the center or ultimate source . . . .

According to these definitions the Bible qualifies as radical from several different perspectives. The word of God deals with the very *root* of things. It contains a *fundamental* message about life, life's *center*, and its *ultimate source*. We believe that the Bible has a powerful message for the world of the 1970s. And so we have selected Scriptural passages and set them with contemporary commentaries on what is happening today.

Our focus has been justice and the Third World. (Roughly, the "Third World" means the poor and powerless peoples of the earth—most of whom live in Asia, Africa, and Latin America.) This is not to say that justice is all that the Bible speaks of, nor that it speaks only of the powerful rich and their frequent oppression of the powerless poor, nor that these Scriptural passages provide neat formulas for dealing with specific contemporary issues.

Our hope is that the confrontation of God's Word with expressions of the problems and aspirations of peoples today will be provocative. We believe that God's Word should jolt us, for "the voice of the Lord breaks down cedars" and "flashes forth flames of fire" (Ps. 29). Ours is a God of radical transformations and rearrangements, the God who puts down the mighty from their thrones and exalts those of low degree (Luke 1).

Our aim is not to prove to the skeptical that the Bible is relevant; rather it is to remind us Christians of what we have consented to.

the radical bible was originally published in Germany as *bibel provokativ.* For the US edition we have preserved most of the Scriptural quotations, but we present a completely new selection of contemporary comments.

John Eagleson
Philip Scharper

1. the world
was made
for everyone

you shall have food

Then God said, "Let us make man in our
image, after our likeness; and let them
have dominion over the fish of the sea,
and over the birds of the air, and
over the cattle, and over all the earth, and
over every creeping thing that creeps upon
the earth." So God created man in his
own image, in the image of God he created
him; male and female he created them. And
God blessed them, and God said to them,
"Be fruitful and multiply, and fill the
earth and subdue it; and have dominion over
the fish of the sea and over the birds of
the air and over every living thing that
moves upon the earth." And God said,
"Behold, I have given you every plant
yielding seed which is upon the face of all
the earth, and every tree with seed in its
fruit; you shall have them for food. . . ."

Genesis 1:26-29

Symbolize the whole three billion people
alive today by a village of 1,000. Only 164
of these can be said to be living a moder-

ately satisfied life. 836 exist under varying degrees of desperation, poverty, disease, economic and political oppressions, conditions of degradation.

J. C. Smith and W. C. Baker in *The Word and the Act*, A Study for Christians on Development of the United Presbyterian Church in the USA, p. 16

God intended the earth and all that it contains for the use of every human being and people. Thus, as all men follow justice and unite in charity, created goods should abound for them on a reasonable basis . . . . A man should regard his lawful possessions not merely as his own but also as common property in the sense that they should accrue to the benefit of not only himself but of others . . . . The right to have a share of earthly goods sufficient for oneself and one's family belongs to everyone . . . . If a person is in extreme necessity, he has the right to take from the riches of others what he himself needs.

Vatican Council II, *The Church in the Modern World*, no. 59

where is your brother?

*Then the Lord said to Cain, "Where is
Abel your brother?" He said, "I do not
know; am I my brother's keeper?" And
the Lord said, "What have you done?
The voice of your brother's blood is crying
to me from the ground . . . . "* Genesis 4:9-10

Since there are deep political reasons why
the US is not "sacrificing" to help the poor
countries and will not do so, then regret-
tably, it is naively optimistic to suggest . . .
that we can have a different kind of development policy by "appealing to peoples'
moral feelings." A nation that can remain
morally indifferent to the poverty of fellow
citizens in Harlem, Appalachia, Mississippi,
or indeed of its own parents in squalid "re-
tirement communities" and "rest homes"
cannot generate much compassion for hungry *campesinos* [peasants] in Brazil.

> R. J. Barnet, Director of the Institute for
> Policy Studies, in *Can the United States
> Promote Foreign Development?*, p. 8

All human beings are born free and equal in dignity and rights. They are endowed with reason and conscience and should act towards one another in a spirit of brotherhood.

United Nations Universal Declaration of Human Rights, Article I

---

god gives everything

And God blessed Noah and his sons, and said to them, "Be fruitful and multiply, and fill the earth . . . . Every moving thing that lives shall be food for you; and as I gave you the green plants, I give you everything."   Genesis 9:1,3

It seems that the slaughterhouse threw kerosene on their garbage dump so the *favelado* [slum dweller] would not look for meat to eat. I didn't have any breakfast and walked around half dizzy. The daze of hunger is worse than that of alcohol. The daze of alcohol makes us sing, but the one of hunger makes us shake. I know how horrible it is to only have air in the stomach.

> *Child of the Dark,* the Diary of Carolina
> Maria de Jesus, a Brazilian slum dweller,
> p. 52

We Christians . . . are ourselves responsible for the misuse of the resources God has given to the world. And our responsibility is not merely as persons for other people, but also for the political and economic structures that bring about poverty, injustice and violence. Today our responsibility has a new dimension because men now have the power to remove the causes of the evil, whose symptoms alone they could treat before.

> Report of the Beirut Conference on World
> Development, sponsored by the World
> Council of Churches and the Pontifical
> Commission Justice and Peace, p. 15

2. israel:
model for mankind

deliverance from oppression

*Then the Lord said, "I have seen the
affliction of my people who are in Egypt,
and have heard their cry because of
their taskmasters; I know their sufferings,
and I have come down to deliver them out
of the hand of the Egyptians, and to
bring them up out of that land to a good
and broad land, a land flowing with milk
and honey. . . . And now, behold, the cry
of the people of Israel has come to me, and
I have seen the oppression with which the
Egyptians oppress them. Come, I will send
you to Pharaoh that you may bring forth my
people, the sons of Israel, out of Egypt."*
Exodus 3:7-10

Never before in history has the disparity between the rich and the poor, the comfort-
able and the starving, been so extreme; never
before have mass communications so vividly
informed the sufferers of the extent of their
misery; never before have the privileged

societies possessed weapons so powerful that their employment in the defense of privilege would destroy the haves and the have-nots indiscriminately. We are faced with an overwhelming challenge.

> Pierre Trudeau, Prime Minister of Canada, in *CERES*, (UN Food and Agricultural Organization Review), September-October 1968

No, it is not God's will that a few rich people enjoy the goods of this world and exploit the poor. No, it is not God's will that some people remain poor and abject forever. No, religion is not the opiate of the people; it is a force that exalts the lowly and casts down the proud, that feeds the hungry and sends the sated away empty.

> "Letter of the Peoples of the Third World," signed by 18 Third World Catholic Bishops, in *Between Honesty and Hope*, p. 10

called to brotherhood

*"When you reap the harvest of your land, you
shall not reap your field to its very border,
neither shall you gather the gleanings after
your harvest. And you shall not strip your
vineyard bare, neither shall you gather the
fallen grapes of your vineyard; you shall
leave them for the poor and for the
sojourner: I am the Lord your God. You
shall not steal, nor deal falsely, nor
lie to one another . . . ."*   Leviticus 19:9-11

*"You shall not oppress your neighbor or
rob him. The wages of a hired servant shall
not remain with you all night until the
morning. You shall not curse the deaf or
put a stumbling block before the blind,
but you shall fear your God: I am
the Lord. You shall do no injustice in
judgment; you shall not be partial to the
poor or defer to the great, but in
righteousness shall you judge your
neighbor . . . ."*   Leviticus 19:13-15

"You shall not take vengeance or bear any grudge against the sons of your own people, but you shall love your neighbor as yourself; I am the Lord . . . ." Leviticus 19:18

In the light of the New Testament, we understand that God's People of the Old Testament were a model: Israel was not chosen from all the other peoples for its own sake, but for the salvation of the world. Being chosen means receiving, and expecting, one's life solely from God. It is not meant for the individual, but for the community—for the individual only as a member of the community. The notably social character of Israelite law is based on this communal election. The right to life which God bestows on his people is meant for all without distinction. There are no privileged persons where God alone is Lord. People become brothers and sisters under the same Father.

you must remember egypt

*"You shall not pervert the justice due to the
sojourner or to the fatherless, or take a
widow's garment in pledge; but you shall
remember that you were a slave in Egypt and
the Lord your God redeemed you from there;
therefore I command you to do this. When
you reap your harvest in your field, and
have forgotten a sheaf in the field, you
shall not go back to get it; it shall be
for the sojourner, the fatherless, and the
widow; that the Lord your God may bless
you in all the work of your hands. When
you beat your olive trees, you shall not go
over the boughs again; it shall be for the
sojourner, the fatherless, and the widow.
When you gather the grapes of your
vineyard, you shall not glean it afterward;
it shall be for the sojourner, the
fatherless, and the widow. You shall remember
that you were a slave in the land of Egypt:
therefore I command you to do this."*

Deuteronomy 24:17-22

We say man was created in the image of God. I refuse to imagine a God who is miserable, poor, ignorant, superstitious, fearful, oppressed and wretched—which is the lot of the majority of those He created in His own image.

Julius K. Nyerere, President of Tanzania, in *Maryknoll* magazine, June 1971, p. 37

I suggest that we are thieves in a way. If I take anything that I do not need for my own immediate use, and keep it, I thieve it from somebody else . . . . In India we have got three millions of people having to be satisfied with one meal a day, and that meal consisting of unleavened bread [*chapati*] containing no fat in it, and a pinch of salt. You and I have no right to anything that we really have until these three millions are clothed and fed better. You and I, who ought to know better, must adjust our wants, and even undergo voluntary starvation in order that they may be nursed, fed and clothed.

Mahatma Gandhi, in *All Men are Brothers*, p. 130

ears that don't hear

He who closes his ear to the cry of
the poor
will himself cry out and not be heard.

Proverbs 21:13

There was once a man who had a rich property. He gave it to his children to care for. Because the father loved his children, he left on a long journey and gave them real freedom to organise his property their own way. Now part of that property was cultivated and another part was not. The sons who lived on the richer part built fences to defend their section from the others who lived on the wild parts. They led a good life themselves, and once in a while threw some food over the fence so that the other children at least knew good life could be. Then the children on the other side of the fence sent a delegation to their brothers and said, "Teach us how to cultivate our soil, and while we learn, share your riches with us so that we do not die." But their brothers said,

14

"Go away: there is not enough for all of us. Learn to till the soil yourselves." The others said, "We will do that, but we have no tools to till the soil. Help us with your tools." But their brothers responded, "We cannot do that, because we need all we have if we want to keep up our standard of living. We'll give you a few tools, and with them you can make your own." The others said, "In order to make tools we need money. Buy what we have reaped on our land and we shall buy our own tools from you." Their brothers replied, "But we don't need products. If you sell them to us our economy will be disrupted." The others said, "But then what shall we do; our wives and our children are dying." Their brothers said, "It will take time." The others, seeing that their brothers did not really want to help them, stormed the fence, broke it down, took the food they needed and killed all the brothers who resisted them. Then the owner of the property returned, and was both angry and sad. To the surprise of the children who had lived behind their fences, he put the others in charge of the whole property and forgave them their violence.

Albert van den Heuvel, Director of the Youth Department of the World Council of Churches, in *Risk,* nos. 1-2, p. 149

In New Delhi at the UN Conference on Trade and Development the Soviet Union and the United States demonstrated once more their incomprehension of, and bad faith toward, the underdeveloped world. It was in vain that the Asian nations met at Bangkok, the African nations at Algiers, and the Latin American nations at Tequendama. It was in vain that the underdeveloped world sent its letter from Algiers, insisting that the problem of relations between the affluent nations and poor countries is not a question of foreign aid but of justice on a worldwide scale. The two superpowers, the supreme embodiments of capitalism on the one hand and socialism on the other, remain deaf and blind to these pleas; they continue to remain closed up in their own egotism.

Dom Helder Camara, Catholic Archbishop of Olinda and Recife, Brazil, in *Between Honesty and Hope*, p. 50

breaking through the vicious circle

"And you shall count seven weeks of years,
seven times seven years, so that the time
of the seven weeks of years shall be to
you forty-nine years. Then you shall send
abroad the loud trumpet on the tenth day of
the seventh month; on the day of atonement
you shall send abroad the trumpet through-
out all your land. And you shall hallow the
fiftieth year, and proclaim liberty
throughout the land to all its inhabitants;
it shall be a jubilee for you, when each of
you shall return to his property and each
of you shall return to his family."

Leviticus 25:8-10

Behind the law concerning the jubilee year
lies the conviction that God has bestowed
the land and its riches on all the people.
Each family had received a just portion in
the partitioning of the land. But the original
equality did not prevent in time the rise of
inequality due to debt or reverses. The jubi-
lee year was meant to re-establish equality of

17

opportunity and to make a new beginning possible for all.

It does not matter whether this law was actually enforced. It follows logically, as a demand, from the call to brotherhood. Today, we have to think not only of the poor of our own nation, but also of the poor of other nations. The vicious circle must be broken. It can be depicted in various ways:

Low output causes low income causes little demand and small savings causes few investments causes low output.

Undernourishment causes ill health causes insufficient energy to work causes little income causes undernourishment.

Deficient training causes joblessness causes no funds for tuition causes deficient training.

This complex multi-causality of underdevelopment can be summarized in the often-used expression "vicious circles." It is not "just" a lack of capital, or "just" backward ways, or "just" a population problem, or even "just" a political problem, which weighs upon the poorer nations. It is a combination of all of these, each aggravating the other. The troubles of underdevelopment feed upon themselves; one cannot easily attack one of the shackles of underdevelopment without contending with them all.

> Robert L. Heilbroner, economic historian, in *The Great Ascent*, p. 72

It is not enough to free man from the hunger imposed on him by an insufficiency of food.

Man must be freed of all the forces that oppress him, of the natural, economic and political order.

> Youth delegates to the Second World Food Congress of the UNFAO, in *IDOC-NA*, no. 9, p. 88

aid without strings

"If you lend money to any of my people with you who is poor, you shall not be to him as a creditor, and you shall not exact interest from him. If ever you take your neighbor's garment in pledge, you shall restore it to him before the sun goes down; for that is his only covering, it is his mantle for his body; in what else shall he sleep? . . . " Exodus 22:25-27

It is a fact, that, as yet, no Western developed nation has made any real sacrifices in shouldering aid obligations to underdeveloped countries. Neither have they been prepared, on the whole, to abstain from even minor trading advantages that can be shown not to be of real long-term interest to a developed country. The trend has not gone in the direction of greater willingness to come to the assistance of the underdeveloped countries.

Gunnar Myrdal, Swedish economist, in *The Challenge of World Poverty*, p. 313

What makes matters more difficult for the new nations is that the older, developed nations do not usually give the kind of aid we want. Aid designed to promote the exports of the donor is bad aid. Aid that is intended directly or indirectly to bribe the recipient into being a satellite or fellow-traveler is bad aid. Aid that is given with an air of condescension is also bad aid. The desirable type of aid is that which is given for the right purpose to the right people for the right things, given with no improper strings.

Chief S. O. Adebo, Representative of Nigeria to the US, in *On the Developed and the Developing*, p. 10

---

disastrous free trade

"And if your brother becomes poor, and cannot maintain himself with you, you shall maintain him; as a stranger and a sojourner he shall live with you. Take no interest from him or increase, but fear your God; that your brother may live beside you. You

shall not lend him your money at interest,
nor give him your food for profit. I am the
Lord your God, who brought you forth out
of the land of Egypt to give you the land of
Canaan, and to be your God."

Leviticus 25:35-38

The efforts being made to help the needy countries to develop are being undone when trade between these countries and the rich is unbalanced. All foreign aid is met with justified suspicion when one hand takes away what the other hand has given. The nations that are industrialized export mostly manufactured goods. Emerging nations normally sell food, fibres and other raw materials. The trouble now is this: the market price of manufactured goods keeps going up. The market price of food and raw materials goes up and down, quite wildly. A sudden fall in prices can wipe out all the gains made by a developing nation. A country which must export to pay for what it needs can be quite crippled in this way. Here is one reason then why the poor stay poor yet see the rich grow richer.

Free trade is not enough to regulate world markets. Free trade can work quite well between two equal partners. Free trade between unequal states can be disastrous.

> Pope Paul VI, Encyclical Letter, *This is Progress*, (Claretian translation), nos. 56-58

Capitalism has set up once more the idols execrated of old by the people of God— mammon, Baal, and Astharte. Filipino Christians have the obligation to smash these idols enshrined in the capitalist structure, both in its foreign neocolonial aspect and in its domestic semi-feudal manifestations. We must set up new alternative political and economic structures that will promote the full human development of our people. We must collaborate in building a new world order wherein men will strive not for selfish gain but for service to the common good of the human race.

> Statement of the Christian Filipino Democratic Movement, July 1971, in *IDOC-NA* no. 33, p. 26

robbing the poor

Do not rob the poor, because he is poor,
or crush the afflicted at the gate.

Proverbs 22:22

Over the past year Tanzania did receive capital assistance from abroad . . . . But it is important that we should understand what it means in real terms and in comparison with our needs. For the truth is that the total amount of external capital aid was less than the amount by which our sisal [fiber] earnings went down because of the fall in international prices . . . . It would have been far better if we had received no aid at all, but the prices of our commodities had not fallen.

Julius K. Nyerere, President of Tanzania,
in Freedom and Socialism, p. 166

We have seen the developed world's financial leaders discuss the future of the whole regime of international trade with barely a mention of the two-thirds of hu-

manity in developing lands who depend upon it for any hope of further advance.

Barbara Ward, British economist, at the
Catholic Bishops Synod in Rome, October 1971

justice for the afflicted

Give justice to the weak and the fatherless;
maintain the right of the afflicted and
the destitute.
Rescue the weak and the needy; deliver them
from the hand of the wicked.

Psalm 82:3-4

Once every four years the politicians change
without solving the problem of hunger that
has its headquarters in the *favela* [slum
quarter] and its branch offices in the
workers homes . . . .

I found a sweet potato and a carrot in the
garbage. When I got back to the *favela* my
boys were gnawing on a piece of hard bread.

I thought for them to eat this bread, they need electric teeth.

Child of the Dark, the Diary of Carolina Maria de Jesus, a Brazilian slum dweller, p. 48

Christians and their pastors should know how to recognize the hand of the Almighty in those events that occur sporadically—when the powerful are dethroned and the lowly are exalted, when the rich are sent away empty-handed and the needy are filled. Today the world insistently calls for recognition of man's full dignity and for social equality among all classes. Christians and all men of good will cannot but go along with this demand, even if it means that they must give up their privileges and their personal fortunes for more equitable distribution in the social community.

"Letter to Peoples of the Third World," signed by 18 Third World Catholic Bishops, in *Between Honesty and Hope*, p. 6

go, tell it on the mountain

*Open your mouth for the dumb, for the
    rights of all who are left desolate.
Open your mouth, judge righteously,
    maintain the rights of the poor
    and needy.*   Proverbs 31:8-9

Christians in our time have allied themselves
with capitalism, colonialism and white racism.

Eugene Carson Blake, General Secretary of
the World Council of Churches, March
1970, in *IDOC-NA*, no. 7, p. 32

It is the duty of the Christian citizen to
stand up and be counted in all matters affecting the public welfare. It is the duty of
the Christian citizen to participate con-
scientiously in the political life of the country. It is his duty to break the silence of the
"silent majority" when injustice is committed, when those in public office fail in
their obligations.

Joint communiqué of the Catholic Bishops
Conference of the Philippines, July 1970,
in *IDOC-NA*, no. 14, p. 64

power

*Again I saw all the oppressions that
are practiced under the sun. And behold,
the tears of the oppressed, and they had no
one to comfort them! On the side of their
oppressors there was power, and there was
no one to comfort them. And I thought the
dead who are already dead more fortunate
than the living who are still alive; but
better than both is he who has not yet been,
and has not seen the evil deeds that are
done under the sun.*   Ecclesiastes 4:1-3

The significance about this division between
rich and poor is not simply that one man has
more food than he can eat, more clothes
than he can wear and more houses than he
can live in, while others are hungry, unclad
or homeless. The significant thing about the
division between rich and poor nations is not
simply that one has the resources to provide
comfort for all its citizens and the other cannot provide basic services.

The reality and the depth of the problem arises because the man who is rich has power over the lives of those who are poor. And the rich nation has power over the policies of those who are not rich. And even more important is that a social and economic system, nationally and internationally, supports those divisions and constantly increases them so that the rich get ever richer and more powerful, while the poor get relatively ever poorer and less able to control their own future.

> Julius K. Nyerere, President of Tanzania, in *Maryknoll* magazine, June 1971, pp. 34-35

The Third World will continue to be controlled by those who are said to be developed, and human degradation will increase—unless radical changes take place in the perspectives and values of the developed.

> James Lamb, Executive Director of the Center for the Study of Development and Social Change, in *The Myth of Aid*, p. 7

empty words

For when dreams increase, empty words grow many: but do you fear God.   Ecclesiastes 5:7

When a politician tells us in his speeches that he is on the side of the people, that he is only in politics in order to improve our living conditions, asking for our votes, promising to freeze prices, he is well aware that by touching on these grave problems he will win at the polls. Afterward he divorces himself from the people. He looks at them with half-closed eyes, and with a pride that hurts us.   *Child of the Dark*, the Diary of Carolina Maria de Jesus, a Brazilian slum dweller, p. 46

Let each one examine himself, to see what he has done up to now, and what he ought to do. It is not enough to recall principles, state intentions, point to crying injustices and utter prophetic denunciations; these words will lack real weight unless they are accompanied for each individual by a livelier awareness of personal responsibility and by effective action. It is too easy to throw back on others responsibility for injustices, if at the same time one does not realize how each one shares in it personally.

Pope Paul VI, Apostolic Letter to Cardinal Maurice Roy, no. 48

3. god is on the side of the oppressed

god's unfaithful people

My beloved had a vineyard
*   on a very fertile hill.*
He digged it and cleared it of stones,
*   and planted it with choice vines;*
he built a watchtower in the midst of it,
*   and hewed out a wine vat in it;*
*   and he looked for it to yield*
*   grapes, but it yielded wild grapes.*
And now, O inhabitants of Jerusalem
*   and men of Judah,*
*   judge, I pray you, between me and*
*   my vineyard.*
What more was there to do for my
*   vineyard,*
*   that I have not done in it?*
When I looked for it to yield grapes,
*   why did it yield wild grapes?*
And now I will tell you what I will do
*   to my vineyard.*
I will remove its hedge,
*   and it shall be devoured;*
I will break down its wall,
*   and it shall be trampled down.*

I will make it a waste;
  it shall not be pruned or hoed,
  and briers and thorns shall grow up
I will also command the clouds that
  they rain no rain upon it.
For the vineyard of the Lord of hosts
  is the house of Israel,
and the men of Judah
  are his pleasant planting;
and he looked for justice,
  but behold, bloodshed;
for righteousness,
  but behold, a cry!   Isaiah 5:1-7

The Law told Israel what God's choice of
them must mean in the life of the people.
What was the reality? The Prophets unani-
mously complained about serious social
abuses: The rich and powerful oppressed and
mercilessly exploited the poor, the weak
man sought his rights in vain before judges
who themselves belonged to or were dependent on the propertied classes. Those responsible could assert in answer to these
reproaches that they were acting under the
force of political and economic necessity.

Actually, it was not only a moral problem, but also a question of the constantly endangered existence of Israel as a state. The introduction of kingship was an attempt to protect the people more effectively against enemies. But it led to the creation of a military and administrative hierarchy and—with the introduction of a money economy—those conditions against which the Prophets protested.

Were the Prophets unworldly Utopians when they appealed to the ancient law of God? Did they oppose inevitable development? Did they close their eyes to the challenges of the times? The Prophets were convinced that no politics could avert the catastrophe which they had to announce as God's judgment over his people. They believed that the very conditions necessary to guarantee Israel's existence as a state were indeed the cause for the destruction of the state. Only a people completely dependent upon the God who chose them and obedient to the divine election would still have a chance for survival.

The situation in which the Prophets spoke to Israel was unique and not to be repeated. But the Prophets challenged once and for all the autonomy of so-called political necessities. The right to life of the weak and powerless is undeniable in every conceivable situation. The brotherhood of all people must be the aim of all politics. The Utopia towards which the Prophets oriented themselves is a Utopia vitally necessary for mankind.

The upsurge of aspirations from the hitherto voiceless and hopeless has come to us as a cry from the depths; the panorama of misery and desperation visible on the faces of the Arabs, Indians, Africans, and Bolivians, who stare at us from the pages of magazines and television screens, has shocked us like a glimpse into the inferno.

Robert L. Heilbroner, economic historian, in *The Great Ascent*, p. 19

Everyone has the right to a standard of living adequate for the health and well-being of himself and of his family, including food, clothing, housing and medical care and necessary social services, and the right to security in the event of unemployment, sickness, disability, widowhood, old age, or other lack of livelihood in circumstances beyond his control.

United Nations Universal Declaration of Human Rights, Article 25

---

woe to those who feel secure

*"Woe to those who are at ease in Zion.
   and to those who feel secure on the
   mountain of Samaria . . . .
O you who put far away the evil day
   and bring near the seat of violence.
Woe to those who lie upon beds of ivory,
   and stretch themselves upon their
   couches, and eat lambs from the flock,
   and calves from the midst of the stall;
who sing idle songs to the sound of the
   harp, and like David invent for themselves instruments of music;*

who drink wine in bowls, and anoint them-
selves with the finest oils,
but are not grieved over the ruin of
Joseph!... Amos 6:1, 3-6

The developed countries should not content
themselves with negative and self-seeking at-
titudes. The present trade pattern, which is
very much to their advantage, cannot last
indefinitely. Sooner or later, the States that
are victims of this lamentable situation must
be expected to revolt, and their revolt will
have the gravest consequences for international peace and security.

Malick Zorome, Minister for Foreign Affairs of Upper Volta, at the United Nations General Assembly

In economic history one has to search rather
diligently to find instances where the
"haves" of the possessing classes have will-
ingly given up any of their privileges. The
"have-nots" had almost invariably to wrest
their rights through agrarian movements,
workers movements, trade-union activity
and so on.

S. L. Parmar, United Church of Northern
India, in *Uppsala Speaks*, p. 42

you have devoured the vineyard

The Lord has taken his place to contend,
*   he stands to judge his people.*
The Lord enters into judgment with the
*   elders and princes of his people:*
"It is you who have devoured the vineyard,
*   the spoil of the poor is in your houses.*
What do you mean by crushing my people,
*   by grinding the face of the poor?" says*
*   the Lord of hosts.*   Isaiah 3:13-15

The history of foreign corporations operating in weak nations is replete with injustice; efficiency, profits, and loyalty to their own country taking priority over the needs and aspirations of local people; taking too much and leaving too little; crushing local competition and gaining monopolistic power; making poor countries dependent on foreign sources for modern technology and even national defense; being instruments of their own country's foreign policy; and creating desires that cannot be satisfied by the poor country.

Alexander Carter, Catholic Bishop of Sault Sainte Marie, Canada, at the Bishops Synod in Rome, October 1971

Once upon a time, [there was] uttered a phrase that has been immortalized in the history of the abolition of slavery in Brazil: "No more slaves will be shipped from this harbor." Latin America will move toward its true autonomy the day when, after a firm, deliberate political decision, its governments say: "No more raw materials will be shipped from this continent." We are sick and tired of selling our raw materials at a trivial price, and then buying them back some months later, for ever-mounting prices, when they have been manufactured.

Dom Helder Camara, Catholic Archbishop of Olinda and Recife, Brazil, in *LADOC*, I, 30

you have trampled upon the poor

Hear this, you who trample upon the needy,
*   and bring the poor of the land to an end*
saying, "When will the new moon be over,
*   that we may sell grain?*
And the sabbath,
*   that we may offer wheat for sale,*
that we may make the ephah small and
*   the shekel great,*
*   and deal deceitfully with false balances,*
that we may buy the poor for
*   silver and the needy*
for a pair of sandals,
*   and sell the refuse of the wheat?"*
The Lord has sworn by the pride of Jacob:
*   "Surely I will never forget any of their*
*   deeds. . . ."*   Amos 8:4-7

Just as water from the driest regions of the earth ultimately flows into the ocean where already there is plenty, so wealth flows from the poorest nations and the poorest individuals into the hands of those nations and those individuals who are already too wealthy. A man who can afford to buy only one loaf of bread a day contributes to the profit accruing to the owner of the bakery despite the fact that the owner already has more money than he knows how to use. And the poor nation which sells its primary commodities on the world market in order to buy machines for development finds that the prices it obtains and the prices it has to pay are both determined by the forces of the free market in which it is a pygmy fighting against giants. For he that hath to him shall be given, and he who hath not that also which he hath shall be taken away from him.

Julius K. Nyerere, President of Tanzania, in *Maryknoll* magazine, June 1971, p. 35

The developing countries do not ask for charity, but for a readjustment of the terms of trade and aid in such a way as to bring prosperity to all. It is within the power of the advanced countries to redress or aggravate the situation, which is a matter for ac-

tion and not merely good intentions and
pious resolutions.

M. T. Mashologu, Chairman of the Delegation of Lesotho, at the United Nations
General Assembly

---

they oppress a man

*Woe to those who devise wickedness and work
    evil upon their beds!*
*When the morning dawns, they perform it,
    because it is in the power of their hand.*
They covet fields, and seize them;
    and houses, and take them away;
    they oppress a man and his house,
    a man and his inheritance.   Micah 2:1-2

More often than not, a peasant would have
to work at least several hundred years in order to earn the annual income of one rich
landlord from one of his estates.

Ernest Feder, of the UN Economic Commission for Latin America, in *CERES*
(FAO Review), November-December
1969, p. 26

I have the audacity to believe that peoples everywhere can have three meals a day for their bodies, education and culture for their minds, and dignity, equality and freedom for their spirits. I believe that what self-centered men have torn down other-centered can build up. I still believe that one day mankind will bow before the altars of God and be crowned triumphant over war and blood-shed, and nonviolent redemptive goodwill will proclaim the rule of the land. "And the lion and the lamb shall lie down together and every man shall sit under his own vine and fig tree and none shall be afraid." I still believe that we shall overcome.

Martin Luther King, Nobel Peace Prize Acceptance Speech

---

your rich men are full of violence

*The voice of the Lord cries to the city —
    and it is sound wisdom to fear thy name:
    "Hear, O tribe and assembly of the city!*

Can I forget the treasures of wickedness in
  the house of the wicked,
    and the scant measure that is accursed?
Shall I acquit the man with wicked scales
  and with a bag of deceitful weights?
Your rich men are full of violence;
  your inhabitants speak lies,
    and their tongue is
    deceitful in their mouth.
Therefore I have begun to smite you,
  making you desolate because of
  your sins. . . ."   Micah 6:9-13

Underdevelopment is a chronic state of violence. This is the reason why the adoption of
a gradualist path to social improvement may
entail much complicity with violence. Revolutions also lead to violence. The first form
of violence is expressed in inhumanly high
birth and death rates, degrading poverty, ignorance, and non-participation in significant
decisions affecting the lives of countless
men. Support given to a more visible and
militant form of violence, revolutionary
activity, likewise involves the loss of life. It

may, nonetheless, prove to be a more ethically sound position than passive complicity in privilege structures which perpetuate injustice and that impersonal, anonymous, and disguised form of violence known as underdevelopment. The problem needs to be diagnosed in terms of a choice not between violence and non-violence—since even the non-violent position allows violence to exist —but between different kinds of violence and different degrees of human complicity with it. "Developed" observers tend to argue that violence is too high a price to pay to obtain development. What they choose to ignore is the high price paid by underdeveloped peoples to remain underdeveloped.

Denis Goulet, development ethician at the Center for the Study of Development and Social Change, in *The Cruel Choice,* p. 317

As the Christian believes in the productiveness of peace in order to achieve justice, he also believes that justice is a prerequisite for peace. He recognizes that in many instances Latin America finds itself faced with a situation of injustice that can be called institutionalized violence, when, because of a structural deficiency of industry and agriculture, of national and international economy, of cultural and political life, whole towns lack necessities, live in such dependence as hinders all initiative and responsibility as well as every possibility for cultural promotion and participation in social and political life, thus violating fundamental rights. This situation demands all-embracing, courageous, urgent and profoundly renovating transformations. We should not be surprised therefore, that the "temptation to violence" is surfacing in Latin America. One should not abuse the patience of a people that for years has borne a situation that would not be acceptable to anyone with any degree of awareness of human rights.

Second General Conference of Latin American Bishops, Medellín, Colombia, 1968, "Peace," no. 16

you have plundered many nations

"Woe to him who heaps up what is not
his own—for how long?—
and loads himself with pledges!"
Will not your debtors suddenly arise,
and those awake who will make you
tremble?
Then you will be booty for them.
Because you have plundered many nations,
all the remnant of the peoples shall
plunder you,
for the blood of men and violence
of the earth,
to cities and all who dwell therein.

Ḥabakkuk 2:6-8

Some of those who call me a subversive, a
Communist, a red, must do so in jest or in
malice. But there are others who really believe it and who pray for my conversion. I
inquired once about the basis for that absurd
accusation. A general explained it to me
thus:

"When you set out to convert the masses

into persons, Bishop, you say that literacy isn't enough, that you want to conscientize them—to open their eyes, make them look at the facts, awaken their initiative, teach them to work together and not wait till city hall acts for them. But don't you see you are unleashing a force that tomorrow you won't be able to control? It is a lot easier to conscientize than to carry out structural reforms. That's why, if you keep on conscientizing the masses, you are a subversive. And since you are setting one class against the other, you are a Communist—or at least you are doing their work."

The answer to the general seems obvious to me. With us, without us, or perhaps despite us, the masses are going to wake up.

Dom Helder Camara, Catholic Archbishop of Olinda and Recife, Brazil, in *LADOC*, I, 30

The longing for a just society is causing revolutions all over the world. Since many Christians are deeply rooted in the *status quo* they tend to be primarily concerned for the maintenance of law and order. Where the maintenance of order is an obstacle to a *just* order, some will decide for revolutionary action against that injustice, struggling for a just society without which the new humanity cannot fully come. The Christian community must decide whether it can recognize the validity of their decision and support them. Fourth Assembly of the World Council of Churches, Uppsala, Sweden, in *Uppsala Speaks,* p. 31

---

your houses shall be desolate

Woe to those who join house to house,
    who add field to field,
until there is no more room,
    and you are made to dwell alone in
    the midst of the land.
The Lord of hosts has sworn in my hearing:
    "Surely many houses shall be desolate,
    large and beautiful houses,
    without inhabitant . . . ."   Isaiah 5:8-9

Is it not violence that [in Latin America today] a man should die of old age at 28, that a woman should not feed the weakest of four children because there is just enough for the three who may survive, that 500 out of 1000 children should die in the country before the age of two, that a maimed mine worker and his family should starve on the pittance of their indemnity, that student protesters should be tortured, that political prisoners should be shot, that half the children of school age should have no school to attend, that millions should be landless while one family owns acres by the millions, that more than half of the adult population should be illiterate, that one third of the national budget should be spent for late-model weaponry, that 80 percent should live on a yearly per capita income of $80?

> Jorge Lara-Braud, Director of the Hispanic-American Institute, Austin, Texas, in *Our Claim on the Future*, p. 125

Rightly understood, development is disorder because it changes existing social and economic relationships, breaks up old institutions to create new, brings about radical alterations in the values and structures of society. If we engage in development through international cooperation we must recognize that basic changes become necessary in developing and developed nations as also in the international economy. "Development is the new name for peace." But development is disorder, it is revolution. Can we attempt to understand this apparently paradoxical situation which would imply that disorder and revolution are the new name for peace?

S. L. Parmar, United Church of Northern India, in Uppsala Speaks, p. 42

fat and lean sheep

"As for you, my flock, thus says the Lord God: Behold, I judge between sheep and sheep, rams and he-goats. Is it not enough for you to feed on the good pasture, that you must tread down with your feet the rest of your pasture; and to drink of clear water, that you must foul the rest with your feet? And must my sheep eat what you have

*trodden with your feet, and drink what you
have fouled with your feet?*

*"Therefore, thus says the Lord God to
them: Behold, I, I myself will judge between
the fat sheep and the lean sheep. Because
you push with side and shoulder, and thrust
at all the weak with your horns, till you
have scattered them abroad, I will save
my flock, they shall no longer be a prey;
and I will judge between sheep and
sheep . . . ."*
Ezekiel 34:17-22

A few examples will show what bigness and
power can do. Military expenditures in
1970, almost all in the USA and Russia,
amounted to over 200 billion dollars; that is
7% of the world's total production; it equals
the total annual income of the billion people
who live in Latin America, South Asia and
the Middle East. It means that about $60
was spent on national security for each person in the world, and $60 is more than the
total annual income of hundreds of millions
of those people. In the same year the richer

countries devoted less than $3 per person to
development aid.

Alexander Carter, Catholic Bishop of
Sault Sainte Marie, Canada, at the Bishops Synod in Rome, October 1971

The Christian with an awakened consciousness wants love to achieve its desired purpose: that those who are hungry today may
eat their bread with dignity, and the thirsty
may satiate their need without humiliation,
and the workers and peasants may receive
the fruit of their labor without exploitation.
And the way to achieve this is the way of
revolution. The Bible energetically exhorts
us: "Let us not love in word or speech but in
deed and in truth" (1 Jn 3:18). For the
Christians with awakened consciousness this
means a commitment to the oppressed
classes in their struggle for liberation.

Gonzalo Castillo-Cárdenas, minister of the
Colombian Presbyterian Church and Vice-
President of Iglesia y Sociedad en America
Latina (ISAL), in *IDOC-NA*, no. 23, p. 32

an uneasy peace

". . . *Their houses shall be turned over*
    to others,
        their fields and wives together;
for I will stretch out my hand against the
        inhabitants of the land," says the Lord.
"For from the least to the greatest of
        them, every one is greedy for unjust
        gain; and from prophet to priest,
        every one deals falsely.
They have healed the wound of my people
        lightly, saying, 'Peace, peace,'
        when there is no peace.
Were they ashamed when they committed
        abomination? No, they were not
        at all ashamed;
        they did not know how to blush.
Therefore they shall fall among
        those who fall;
        at the time that I punish them,
        they shall be overthrown,"
        says the Lord.   Jeremiah 6:12-15

The affluent white race is thus basically peace oriented, while the colored races, in the wake of their decolonization, are basically justice oriented. Within this context, the peace that the white man seeks seems to the others to be nothing but the perpetuation of the injustices imposed upon them by the social, economic, and political structures of a white dominated world. On the other hand, the desire for justice by the nonwhite world is seen by the white race as nothing short of a socio-economic revolution. The conflict of interest is thus inevitable.

> Daisuke Kitagawa, Japan, of the Division of World Mission and Evangelism of the World Council of Churches, in *The Maze of Peace*, p. 80

In considering the problem of violence in Latin America, let us by all means avoid equating the *unjust violence* of the oppressors (who maintain this despicable system) with the *just violence* of the oppressed (who feel obliged to use it to achieve their liberation).

> Statement of 900 Latin American Catholic Priests, in *Between Honesty and Hope*, p. 84

your strongholds shall be plundered

Proclaim to the strongholds in Assyria
and to the strongholds in the
land of Egypt,
and say, "Assemble yourselves upon the
mountains of Samaria,
and see the great tumults within her,
and the oppressions in her midst."
"They do not know how to do right,"
says the Lord,
"those who store up violence and robbery
in their strongholds."
Therefore thus says the Lord God:
"An adversary shall surround the land,
and bring down your defences from you,
and your strongholds shall be plundered."

Amos 3:9-11

When I was on Pedro Vicente Street, the watchman at the junk yard called me and said that I was to go and look for some bags of paper that were near the river.

I thanked him and went to find the sacks. They were bags of rice that had rotted in a warehouse and were thrown away. I was shocked seeing that wasted rice. I stared at the bugs that were there, and the cockroaches and rats that ran from one side to another.

I thought: Why is the white man so perverse? He has money, buys and stores rice away in the warehouse. He keeps playing with the people just like a cat with a rat.

> *Child of the Dark,* the Diary of Carolina Maria de Jesus, a Brazilian slum dweller, pp. 149-150

We speak today of "developing countries" and no longer of "under-developed countries." But for the majority of the Third World there is no prospect of development sufficient even partially to fill the gap separating them from the wealthier world. Countries are stagnating or even retrogressing. It is wrong to think that the Third World is overlooking the hardships of development or that it refuses to follow the rough road leading there. It is unthinkable that in the not too distant future more than three quarters ot mankind will passively accept the growing inequality in the distribution of wealth.

The solution lies in international solidarity. The great Powers, however, are more concerned with the conquest of outer space or with implementing their nuclear arms programmes than with the hunger and misery of the Third World.

Huot Sambath, Permanent Representative of Cambodia, at the United Nations General Assembly

---

establish justice

Seek good, and not evil,
*   that you may live;*
and so the Lord, the God of hosts,
*   will be with you, as you have said.*
Hate evil, and love good,
*   and establish justice in the gate;*
it may be that the Lord, the God of hosts,
*   will be gracious to the remnant*
*   of Joseph.*   Amos 5:14-15

We have ceased to think only of the justice
that awaits us beyond the grave. The sufferings of a famished, sick and exploited mankind, deprived of hope and voice, oblige us
to lay stress on justice in this world. There is
no need to discuss the murderous economic
exploitation exercised by the dominant
social classes; it is a fact known to all.

> Executive Committee of Iglesia y Sociedad
> en América Latina (ISAL), Bolivia, a Divi-
> sion of the World Council of Churches, in
> *IDOC-NA* no. 17, p. 27

Christians are totally committed to the unity
and equality of all mankind under the head-
ship of Christ, the Son of Man, and hence to
unity and justice in the world society in
which the human family lives.

> Report of the Beirut Conference on World
> Development, sponsored by the World
> Council of Churches and the Pontifical
> Commission Justice and Peace, p. 9

desecration of the temple

*The word that came to Jeremiah from the
Lord: "Stand in the gate of the Lord's
house, and proclaim there this word, and
say, Hear the word of the Lord, all you
men of Judah who enter these gates to
worship the Lord. Thus says the Lord of
hosts, the God of Israel, Amend your ways
and your doings, and I will let you dwell
in this place. Do not trust in these
deceptive words: 'This is the temple of
the Lord, the temple of the Lord,
the temple of the Lord.'*

*"For if you truly amend your ways and
your doings, if you truly execute justice
one with another, if you do not oppress the
alien, the fatherless or the widow, or shed
innocent blood in this place, and if you
do not go after other gods to your own
hurt, then I will let you dwell in this
place, in the land that I gave of old to
your fathers for ever.*

*"Behold, you trust in deceptive words
to no avail. Will you steal, murder, commit*

adultery, swear falsely, burn incense to
Baal, and go after other gods that you
have not known, and then come and stand
before me in this house, which is called
by my name, and say, 'We are delivered!'
—only to go on doing all these abominations?
Has this house, which is called by my
name, become a den of robbers in your
eyes? Behold, I myself have seen it, says
the Lord . . . . "   Jeremiah 7:1-11

It is within the framework of paternalism that many people, including Church authorities, approach present-day realities and social problems. They attempt to solve them by appealing to the duty of fraternal charity. They establish countless charitable organizations, social programs, and money campaigns. They unwisely launch philanthropic initiatives that are dear to the middle class, because the latter can thereby work off their feeling of guilt and the responsibility they bear for the gap which separates their standard of living from that of the impoverished people around them. People try to

alleviate the effects produced without tack-
ling the causes behind them. In practice, the
Church's life of action makes her an ac-
complice in the brutal exploitation of the
people and in the misguided effort to solve
poverty and illness on an individual basis.

Statement of 300 Brazilian Priests, in *Between Honesty and Hope*, p. 134

We resolve also to have the courage to speak
out for the rights of the disadvantaged and
powerless, against all forms of injustice no
matter from what source such abuse may
come; we will not tie our hands by com-
promising entanglements with the rich and
the powerful in our respective countries.

Message of the Catholic Asian Bishops
Conference, Manila, 1970, no. 20

---

you tear the skin from my people

Hear, you heads of Jacob
  and rulers of the house of Israel!

Is it not for you to know justice?—
   you who hate the good and love the evil
who tear the skin from off my people,
   and their flesh from off their bones;
who eat the flesh of my people . . . .
Then they will cry to the Lord,
   but he will not answer them;
he will hide his face from them at that time,
   because they have made their deeds evil.
Micah 3:1-4

A big landowner invited me to celebrate Mass at his establishment. All his workers were there, hundreds of them. If I preach and say, for example, that one must obey one's employer, that one must work with patience and goodwill and do one's duty, for this landowner I am "a tremendous bishop," "a holy bishop." I can expect to be invited again to preach. But if, while speaking of the worker's duty and the landowner's rights, I have the audacity, yes the audacity, to mention the worker's rights and the landowner's duty, then it is quite a different matter.

"This is a revolutionary, a progressive, he is pro-communist. . . ."

> Dom Helder Camara, Catholic Archbishop of Olinda and Recife, Brazil, in *The Church and Colonialism*, p. 43

Everyone . . . is entitled to realization . . . of the economic, social and cultural rights indispensable for his dignity and the free development of his personality.

> *United Nations Universal Declaration of Human Rights*, Article 22

---

lip service

"I hate, I despise your feasts,
*   and I take no delight in your*
*   solemn assemblies . . . .*
Take away from me the noise of
*   your songs;*
*   to the melody of your harps I*
*   will not listen.*
But let justice roll down like waters,
*   and righteousness like an*
*   everflowing stream . . . ."* Amos 5:21, 23-24

"Is such the fast that I choose,
    a day for a man to humble himself?
Is it to bow down his head like a rush,
    and to spread sackcloth and ashes
    under him?
Will you call this a fast,
    and a day acceptable to the Lord?
Is not this the fast that I choose:
    to loose the bonds of wickedness,
    to undo the thongs of the yoke,
to let the oppressed go free,
    and to break every yoke?
Is it not to share your bread with
    the hungry,
    and bring the homeless poor into
    your house;
when you see the naked, to cover him,
    and not to hide yourself from
    your own flesh? . . ."   Isaiah 58:5-7

"Not every one who says to me,
'Lord, Lord,' shall enter the kingdom
of heaven, but he who does the will of
my Father who is in heaven. . . ."

                                    Matthew 7:21

4. the kingdom of peace—
a utopia?

the just king: a pious wish?

Give the king thy justice, O God,
*   and thy righteousness to the royal son!*
May he judge thy people with righteousness,
*   and thy poor with justice!*
*   Let the mountains bear prosperity*
*   for the people,*
*   and the hills, in righteousness!*
May he defend the cause of the poor
*   of the people,*
*   give deliverance to the needy,*
*   and crush the oppressor! . . .*
May all kings fall down before him,
*   all nations serve him!*
For he delivers the needy when he calls,
*   the poor and him who has no helper.*
He has pity on the weak and the needy,
*   and saves the lives of the needy.*
From oppression and violence he
*   redeems their life;*
*   and precious is their blood in*
*   his sight . . . .*
May his name endure for ever,
*   his fame continue as long as the sun!*
May men bless themselves by him,
*   all nations call him blessed!*

Psalm 72:1-4, 11-14, 17

The call of the Prophets for social justice
remained unheard. Political and economic
"necessities" prevailed—although they were
not to avert catastrophe. Did God's purpose
for his people fail? Is brotherhood as a
standard of relationships among people an
unattainable ideal? The Psalmist looked to a
future in which justice and politics would no
longer be irreconcilable. He could hope for
this future because he trusted God to carry
out his intention. But when he prayed for
the just king, he knew that God would
achieve his purpose through people.

___

a new world

"For behold, I create new heavens and
*   a new earth;*
and the former things shall not be
*   remembered or come into mind.*
But be glad and rejoice for ever
*   in that which I create. . . .*
No more shall there be in it an infant that
*   lives but a few days,*

or an old man who does not fill out
his days,
for the child shall die a hundred
years old,
and the sinner a hundred years old
shall be accursed.
They shall build houses and inhabit them;
they shall plant vineyards and eat
their fruit.
They shall not build and another inhabit;
they shall not plant and another eat;
for like the days of a tree shall the days
of my people be,
and my chosen shall long enjoy the work
of their hands.
They shall not labor in vain,
or bear children for calamity;
for they shall be the offspring of
the blessed of the Lord.
and their children with them.
Before they call I will answer, while they
are yet speaking I will hear.
The wolf and the lamb shall feed together,
the lion shall eat straw like the ox;
and the dust shall be the serpent's food.
They shall not hurt or destroy in all my
holy mountain, says the Lord."

Isaiah 65: 17-18, 20-25

In this prophetic vision the God of Israel becomes the guarantor of human hope. The expectation of a better future can fill the suffering with consolation and confidence; but it can also tempt us to lose sight of the tasks of the present. Hope for a future in which no more children die can be a sin if meanwhile we neglect to do our best for dying and hopelessly undernourished children today.

When I got out of bed, Vera was already awake and she asked me:

"Mama, isn't today my birthday?"

"It is. My congratulations. I wish you happiness."

"Are you going to make a cake for me?"

"I don't know. If I can get some money . . . ."

I lit the fire and went to carry water. The women were complaining that the water was running out slow.

The garbagemen have gone by. I got little paper. I went by the factory to pick up some rags. I began to feel dizzy. I made up my mind to go to Dona Angelina's house to ask for a little coffee. Dona Angelina gave me some. When I went out I told her I was feeling better.

"It's hunger. You need to eat."

"But what I earn isn't enough."

I have lost eight kilos. I have no meat on my bones, and the little I did have has gone. I picked up the papers and went out. When I went past a shop window I saw my reflection. I looked the other way because I thought I was seeing a ghost.

I fried fish and made some corn mush for the children to eat with the fish. When Vera showed up and saw the mush inside the pot she asked:

"Is that a cake? Today is my birthday!"

"No it isn't cake. It's mush."

"I don't like mush!"

I got some milk. I gave her milk and mush. She ate it, sobbing.

Who am I to make a cake?

Child of the Dark, the Diary of Carolina Maria de Jesus, a Brazilian slum dweller, p. 181

Everyone who works has the right to just and favorable remuneration insuring for himself and his family an existence worthy of human dignity . . . .

United Nations Universal Declaration of Human Rights, Article 23

---

opium or dynamite?

*There shall come forth a shoot
   from the stump of Jesse,
   and a branch shall grow out of his roots.
And the Spirit of the Lord shall rest
   upon him,
   the spirit of wisdom and understanding,
   the spirit of counsel and might,
   the spirit of knowledge and the fear
   of the Lord.
And his delight shall be in the fear
   of the Lord.
He shall not judge by what his eyes see,
   or decide by what his ears hear;
but with righteousness he shall judge
   the poor,*

and decide with equity for the meek
of the earth;
and he shall smite the earth with the
rod of his mouth,
and with the breath of his lips he shall
slay the wicked.
Righteousness shall be the girdle of
his waist,
and faithfulness the girdle of his loins.
The wolf shall dwell with the lamb,
and the leopard shall lie down with the kid,
and the calf and the lion and fatling together,
and a little child shall lead them.
The cow and the bear shall feed;
their young shall lie down together;
and the lion shall eat straw like the ox.
The sucking child shall play over
the hole of the asp,
and the weaned child shall put his hand
on the adder's den.
They shall not hurt or destroy
in all my holy mountain;
for the earth shall be full of the
knowledge of the Lord
as the waters cover the sea.

Isaiah 11:1-9

A world in which peace reigns in every conceivable and desirable sense of the word, a ruler representing the quintessence of justice: Doesn't this vision seem to be anything but "radical"? Some consider it to be simply a product of helpless wishing. And this vision has never caused any of the powerful of the land, whose loss of power is implied here, one sleepless hour. The opium of the people?

The question is put more pointedly in view of the New Testament message. The Prophets of the Old Testament fought for the enforcement of justice in this world. The New Testament community awaits justice from a new world which God will create. But does one who awaits such a future have any reason to fight for the humanization of conditions in this world?

The awaited future is still to come. The majority of Christians have been able to reconcile themselves to the continuation of this imperfect world. We have not seriously quarreled with it. Is it sufficient to settle down in this world and await the solution of all problems on Judgment Day? Whoever thinks that way turns Christian hope into a shabby pacifier and God into a makeshift excuse for his own failure. What did Paul mean when he wrote to Rome, "I consider that the sufferings of this present time are not worth comparing with the glory that is to be revealed to us"? (Rom. 8:18)

The New Testament contains not opium, but dynamite—a message with a revolutionary explosive power. The new world began with Christ, in the midst of this world. We must join the world-renewing movement proceeding from Christ. The message of the Kingdom of God should activate not only our hope, but all our energies as well; we must build the world toward the awaited future, toward the promised final condition.

Christians, Catholics, seem to be stoic spectators of the fall of the world, the world which they abhor. They do not join the struggle. They believe that in the words "my kingdom is not of this world" "world" means "present life" and not "sinful life," as it really does. They forget the prayer of Christ to the Father: "I do not ask that you remove them from the world but that you preserve them from evil." Often we become detached from the world but do not preserve ourselves from evil.

> Camilo Torres, Colombian revolutionary and laicized Catholic priest, in *Revolutionary Writings,* p. 168

Our task is to work for the expression of God's reconciliation here and now. We are not required to wait for a distant "heaven" where all problems will have been solved. What Christ has done, he has done already. We can accept his work or reject it; we can hide from it or seek to live by it. But we cannot postpone it, for it is already achieved. And we cannot destroy it, for it is the work of the eternal God.

> "Message to the South African People" of the theological commission of the Council of African Churches, in *IDOC-NA*, no. 2, pp. 92-93

5. a new beginning

what shall we do?

*. . . The word of God came to John the son
of Zechariah in the wilderness; and he went
into all the region about the Jordan,
preaching a baptism of repentance for the
forgiveness of sins. As it is written in
the book of the words of Isaiah the
prophet,*
> *"The voice of one crying in the
>   wilderness:*
> *Prepare the way of the Lord,*
> *make his paths straight.*
> *Every valley shall be filled,*
> *and every mountain and hill shall
>   be brought low,*
> *and the crooked shall be made
>   straight,*
> *and the rough ways shall be made
>   smooth;*
> *and all flesh shall see the salvation
>   of God."*

*He said therefore to the multitudes that
came out to be baptized by him, "You
brood of vipers! Who warned you to flee*

*from the wrath to come? Bear fruits that
befit repentance, and do not begin to
say to yourselves, 'We have Abraham as
our father'; for I tell you, God is able
from these stones to raise up children
to Abraham. Even now the ax is laid to
the root of the trees; every tree
therefore that does not bear good fruit
is cut down and thrown into the fire."
    And the multitudes asked him, "What
then shall we do?" And he answered
them, "He who has two coats, let him
share with him who has none; and he who
has food, let him do likewise."* Luke 3:2-11

We do not despair in spite of the resistance
of men and structures, with all their delays
and frustrations, because we know that it is
God's world, and that in Christ there is forgiveness and the chance to begin anew every
day, step by step. God wants the world to
develop and He conquers and will conquer
sin. Report of the Beirut Conference on World
Development, sponsored by the World
Council of Churches and the Pontifical
Commission Justice and Peace, p. 17

We do not want to throw the burden of responsibility for the failure of Asian Christianity to identify with the poor entirely on
the official Church. We, the youth, partic-
ularly those who are university students,
have identified ourselves more with bour-
geois classes of society. We have looked for
our own comfort, our security. Even when
we were concerned it was more of an intel-
lectual nature than a commitment which involved a life struggle. We have shied away
from the consequences of living up to the
message of the Gospel in our own local institutions. We have not identified with those
who want to uplift the underprivileged
through a social revolution; while we confess
our failure, we are resolved to be different in
the future.

Pan Asian Conference of Pax Romana,
Hong Kong, in *World Parish* (Maryknoll,
N.Y.), May-June 1971

The God whom we know in the Bible is a
liberating God, a God who destroys myths
and alienations, a God who intervenes in his-

tory in order to break down the structures
of injustice and who raises up prophets in
order to point out the way of justice and
mercy. He is the God who liberates slaves
(Exodus), who causes empires to fall and
raises up the oppressed (Luke 1:52).

Bishop Mortimer Arias, speaking for the
Methodist Evangelical Church in Bolivia,
in *IDOC-NA*, no. 7, p. 42

---

it began with jesus of nazareth

*And he came to Nazareth, where he had been
brought up; and he went to the synagogue,
as his custom was, on the sabbath day. And
he stood up to read; and there was given
to him the book of the prophet Isaiah. He
opened the book and found the place where
it was written,*
    "The Spirit of the Lord is upon me,
    because he has anointed me to preach
        good news to the poor.
    He has sent me to proclaim release to
        the captives
    and recovering of sight to the blind,

> to set at liberty those who are
> oppressed,
> to proclaim the acceptable year
> of the Lord."

*And he closed the book, and gave it back
to the attendant, and sat down; and the
eyes of all in the synagogue were fixed on
him. And he began to say to them, "Today
this scripture has been fulfilled in
your hearing."*
Luke 4:16-21

The Incarnation broke the wall between
time and eternity, temple and market,
church and shop, sacred and secular. The Incarnation allows no division of the Gospel
into personal and social, permits no sur-
render of the group to the devil in order to
rescue one member of it from him, lets no
public injustice escape the Gospel's judgment while the Gospel tends some private
man's grief. The God who assumed flesh
sought the redemption of the whole man in
all his circumstances and conditions. For-

getting this, the Church ceases to be the Church of the Incarnated Christ.

K. Haselden, editor of *The Christian Century*, in *What's Ahead for the Churches?*, pp. 204-05

Even though the Church has talked of developing the whole man to his maximum potentialities, when an attempt is made to put that commitment on record you hear a different tune in Europe and America: "We are interested in welfare. Our responsibility is limited to being the ambulance at the bottom of the cliff, picking up the casualities of the slavery in South Africa or the colonial war in Portuguese territories—Guinea-Biseau, Angola, Mozambique—or the racism in Rhodesia. It's not to be engaged in the task of liberation and freedom." I say this is a distortion of what the Church is about. God's intervention in human history is not to endorse man's powerlessness. He came to take his position with them in order to free them.

Canon Burgess Carr, Liberia, Secretary General of the All Africa Conference of Churches, in *Maryknoll* magazine, January 1972, p. 29

jesus sides with the poor

*And he lifted up his eyes on his
disciples, and said,*

*"Blessed are you poor, for yours is
the kingdom of God.*

*"Blessed are you that hunger
now, for you shall be satisfied.*

*"But woe to you the rich,
for you have received your consolation.*

*"Woe to you that are full now, for
you shall hunger.*

*"Woe to you that laugh now, for you
shall mourn and weep. . . ."*

Luke 6:20-21, 24-25

The children eat a lot of bread. They like
soft bread but when they don't have it, they
eat hard bread.

Hard is the bread that we eat. Hard is the
bed on which we sleep. Hard is the life of
the *favelado*.

Oh, São Paulo! A queen that vainly shows
her skyscrapers that are her crown of gold.

All dressed up in velvet and silk but with cheap stockings underneath—the *favela*.

The money didn't stretch far enough to buy meat, so I cooked macaroni with a carrot. I didn't have any grease, it was horrible. Vera was the only one who complained yet asked for more.

"Mama, sell me to Dona Julita, because she has delicious food."

> *Child of the Dark,* the Diary of Carolina Maria de Jesus, a Brazilian slum dweller, p. 49

From the viewpoint of doctrine, the Church knows that the Gospel calls for the first and most radical revolution: conversion, the thorough-going transformation from sin to grace, from egotism to love, from haughtiness to humble service. This conversion is not simply interior and spiritual; it involves the whole man corporeally and socially as well as spiritually and personally. It has a communitarian aspect that is fraught with consequences for society as a whole. It concerns not only our life on earth but also our eternal life in Christ, who is drawing all men to himself on high.

In her journey through history on earth, however, the Church has almost always been tied up with the political, social, and economic *system* which, at a given moment, insured the common good or at least a certain social order. On the other hand, churches have been seen to be so tied up with the *system*, that they seemed to be wedded to it in marriage. But the Church is not wedded to any system, whatever it might be. It is not now wedded to the "international imperialism of money" any more that it was wedded to royalism or feudalism in the past or will be wedded to some form of socialism in the future. "Letter to Peoples of the Third World," signed by 18 Third World Catholic Bishops, in *Between Honesty and Hope*, pp. 4-5

The Word of God testified that Christ takes the side of the poor and oppressed. We Christians who have not always taken sides as he did, now see a world-wide struggle for economic justice. We should work to vindicate the right of the poor and oppressed and to establish economic justice among the nations and within each state.

Fourth Assembly of the World Council of Churches, Uppsala, Sweden, in *Uppsala Speaks*, p. 61

---

liberated to brotherhood

He entered Jericho and was passing through. And there was a man named Zacchaeus; he was a chief tax collector, and rich. And he sought so see who Jesus was, but could not, on account of the crowd, because he was small of stature. So he ran on ahead and climbed up into a sycamore tree to see him, for he was to pass that way. And when Jesus came to the place, he looked up and said to him, "Zacchaeus, make haste and come down; for I must stay at your house today." So he made haste and came down, and received him joyfully. And when they saw it they all murmured, "He has gone in to be the guest of a man who is a sinner." And Zacchaeus stood

*and said to the Lord, "Behold, Lord, the
half of my goods I give to the poor; and
if I have defrauded any one of anything,
I restore it fourfold." And Jesus said to
him, "Today salvation has come to this
house, since he also is a son of Abraham.
For the Son of man came to seek and to
save the lost."* Luke 19:1-10

*The tax collector understood that the salva-
tion Jesus brings is not a private affair. With
his giving and reparation he proved that he
realized he was once again a part of the people which had been called by God to
brotherhood.*

The presence and the activity of the Church
have inescapable political implications, for
there can be no evangelization without a
commitment to the struggle against domina-
tion. Our pastoral approach cannot remain
on a doctrinal and explanatory level. There
must be an authentic assimilation of the
Gospel that transforms our lives. The Gospel
does not encourage an evasion of our earthly

responsibilities; rather it leads us to assume them and live them before the Lord.

Peruvian Catholic Bishops pre-Synod Statement, 1971, no. 30, in *NADOC*, no. 220

There is no turning to God which does not at the same time bring a man face to face with his fellow men in a new way.

Fourth Assembly of the World Council of Churches, Uppsala, Sweden, in *Uppsala Speaks*, p. 28

What Hollywood films do not explain is that the civilization of the automobile, private swimming pool, air conditioning, private airplane, material comfort and waste of material things is not only based on the ideal of progress and virtues of private enterprise, but also on the exploitation of the mines and plantations of the Third World: a world where low wages and low selling prices of basic products are the reason for the prosperity of 200 million people in the United States.

Claude Julien, French social scientist, in *America's Empire*, p. 310

who is my neighbor?

*And behold, a lawyer stood up to put him to
the test, saying, "Teacher, what shall I
do to inherit eternal life?" He said to
him, "What is written in the law? How do
you read?" And he answered, "You shall
love the Lord your God with all your heart,
and with all your soul, and with all your
strength, and with all your mind; and your
neighbor as yourself." And he said to
him, "You have answered right; do this,
and you will live."*

*But he, desiring to justify himself,
said to Jesus, "And who is my neighbor?"
Jesus replied, "A man was going down from
Jerusalem to Jericho, and he fell among
robbers, who stripped him and beat him,
and departed, leaving him half-dead. Now
by chance a priest was going down the
road; and when he saw him he passed by on
the other side. So likewise a Levite,
when he came to the place and saw him,
passed by on the other side. But a*

Samaritan, as he journeyed, came to
where he was; and when he saw him, he had
compassion, and went to him and bound up
his wounds, pouring on oil and wine; then
he set him on his own beast and brought him
to an inn, and took care of him. And the
next day he took out two denarii and gave
them to the innkeeper, saying, 'Take care
of him; and whatever more you spend, I will
repay you when I come back.' Which of these
three, do you think, proved neighbor to the
man who fell among the robbers?" He said,
"The one who showed mercy on him."
And Jesus said to him, "Go and do
likewise."   Luke 10:25-37

There is no limit to extending our services to our neighbors across State-made frontiers. God never made those frontiers.

> Mahatma Gandhi, in *All Men are Brothers*, p. 121

I refuse to accept the idea that man is mere flotsam and jetsam in the river of life which surrounds him. I refuse to accept the view that mankind is so tragically bound to the starless midnight of racism and war that the bright daybreak of peace and brotherhood can never become a reality .... I believe that wounded justice, lying prostrate on the blood-flowing streets of our nations, can be lifted from this dust of shame to reign supreme among the children of men .... When our days become dreary with low-hovering clouds and our nights become darker than a thousand midnights, we will know that we are living in the creative turmoil of a genuine civilization struggling to be born.

Martin Luther King, Nobel Peace Prize Acceptance Speech

When we look at our Bolivian reality with the eyes of the Gospel, we find ourselves confronted with the spectacle of a chronic and heartrending dehumanization: a country of immense resources sunk in backwardness and underdevelopment; a country living in underconsumption with the lowest per capita income of all Latin America, "the cemeteries of the miners," macabre witnesses of generations sacrificed in the prime of life, leaving, after eight or ten years of production, their skeletons and families of orphans and widows abandoned to the most abject helplessness, while the minerals extracted with the sacrifice of their lives enrich a certain few and strengthen the industry and the finances of the rich nations of the earth; three million peasants, the basic population of the nation, still set apart by illiteracy and poverty and treated as mere disposable objects by political bossism and by the insensitive bureaucracy.

Bishop Mortimer Arias, speaking for the Methodist Evangelical Church in Bolivia, in *IDOC-NA*, no. 7, p. 43

---

crumbs from the table

"There was a rich man, who was clothed in purple and fine linen and who feasted sumptuously every day. And at his gate lay a poor man named Lazarus, full of sores. The poor man died and was carried by the angels to Abraham's bosom. The rich man also died and was buried; and in Hades,

*being in torment, he lifted up his eyes, and
saw Abraham far off and Lazarus in his
bosom. And he called out, 'Father Abraham,
have mercy upon me, and send Lazarus to dip
the end of his finger in water and cool
off my tongue; for I am in anguish in this
flame.' But Abraham said, 'Son, remember
that you in your lifetime received your
good things, and Lazarus in like manner
evil things; but now he is comforted here,
and you are in anguish. And besides all
this, between us and you a great chasm has
been fixed, in order that those who
would pass from here to you may not be
able, and none may cross from there to
us.' And he said, 'Then I beg you,
father, to send him to my father's
house, for I have five brothers, so that
he may warn them, lest they also come
into this place of torment.' But Abraham
said, 'They have Moses and the prophets;
let them hear them.' And he said, 'No,
father Abraham; but if some one goes to
them from the dead, they will repent.'
He said to him, 'If they do not hear
Moses and the prophets, neither will they*

*be convinced if some one should rise
from the dead.' "* Luke 16:19-31

One has risen from the dead, and the rich
confess this at their table, and yet poor
Lazarus, in millions, continues to hunger at
their door. The point of this parable is not,
as is often suspected, the consoling pipe-
dream of heaven for poor Lazarus. It is ad-
dressed exclusively to the rich man. It is not
meant to console the poor with the hope of
recompense beyond the grave, but to warn
the rich of damnation and to incite them to
hear and act in this world.

> Helmut Gollwitzer, German theologian,
> *The Rich Christians and Poor Lazarus,*
> p. 2

The dominantly "white" nations are those
with the most "Christian" tradition, and are
most often identified with the oppressor and
seen as the enemy of the poor.

> J. C. Smith and W. C. Baker in *The Word
> and the Act,* A Study for Christians on
> Development of the United Presbyterian
> Church in the USA, p. 16

... It is not permissible to restrict love to the interpersonal sphere of the I-Thou. Nor is it enough to understand love as charitable work within a neighborhood. We must interpret love, and make it effective, in its societal dimension. This means that love should be the unconditional determination to bring justice, liberty, and peace *to the others*. Thus understood, love contains a socio-critical dynamism . . . .

If love is actualized as the unconditional determination to freedom and justice for the others, there might be circumstances where love itself could demand actions of a *revolutionary character*. If the status quo of a society contains as much injustice as would probably be caused by a revolutionary upheaval, a revolution in favor of freedom and justice for the sake of "the least of our brothers" would be permissible even in the name of love.

Johann Baptist Metz, German theologian, in *Theology of the World,* pp. 118-20

the poor rich man

And he told them a parable, saying,
"The land of a rich man brought forth
plentifully, and he thought to himself,
'What shall I do, for I have nowhere to
store my crops?' And he said, 'I will do
this: I will pull down my barns, and build
larger ones; and there I will store all
my grain and my goods. And I will say to
my soul, Soul, you have ample goods laid
up for many years; take your ease, eat,
drink, be merry.' But God said to him,
'Fool! This night your soul is required of
you; and the things you have prepared,
whose will they be?' . . ."   Luke 12:16-20

What, after all, is the end, the objective, of
development? It is not simply to make
everybody richer and richer. The affluent
societies of the world—choked with the
fumes of their automobiles, threatened with
the poison of industrial waste dumped into
their rivers, their citizens increasingly dis-

traught by the strain inflicted on their nerves—show the blind alley into which that can lead.

Addeke H. Boerma, Director General of the UNFAO at the First Asian Congress of Nutrition, January 1971, in *IDOC-NA*, no. 25, p. 72

The majority of Christians live in the developed North and if this area is wealthy far beyond the general level of world society, they profit from this unbalanced prosperity and must in conscience account for their stewardship.

Report of the Beirut Conference on World Development, sponsored by the World Council of Churches and the Pontifical Commission Justice and Peace, p. 9

---

painless sacrifices

And he sat down opposite the treasury, and watched the multitude putting money into the treasury. Many rich people put in large sums. And a poor widow came, and put

*in two copper coins, which make a penny.
And he called his disciples to him, and
said to them, "Truly, I say to you, this
poor widow has put in more than all those
who are contributing to the treasury. For
they all contributed out of their
abundance; but she out of her poverty has
put in everything she had, her whole
living."*   Mark 12:41-44

A number of the wealthiest nations appear
steadily less committed, less concerned, and
less inventive in their approach to world development.

Barbara Ward, British economist, at the
Catholic Bishops Synod in Rome, October
1971

The best contribution the US can make to
the problem of world poverty is to abandon
or revise many policies it is currently pur-
suing in the name of development that have
the effect of perpetuating misery in the undeveloping world. It is much more exciting
and far less "sacrificial" to conceive and
fund imaginative "projects" than to change

policies that preserve American wealth and power at the expense of poor countries. Any serious commitment to development by the United States, however, would begin by confronting instead of hiding the deep conflicts of interest between Americans, struggling to maintain and increase an unparalleled level of prosperity, and the people of the undeveloping world who are struggling for survival and dignity. We need to find out what it would cost the United States in comfort, convenience, and prosperity to change policies that keep poor countries poor.

Richard J. Barnet, Director of the Institute for Policy Studies, in *Can the United States Promote Foreign Development?*, p. 30

---

hard sayings

"No one can serve two masters; for either he will hate the one and love the other, or he will be devoted to the one and despise the other. You cannot serve God and mammon. . . ." Matthew 6:24

*". . . Again I tell you, it is easier for
a camel to go through the eye of a needle
than for a rich man to enter the kingdom
of God."*   Matthew 19:24

Can we neutralize these words by saying that
it depends on the intention? A rich man can
be spiritually free of his possessions and a
poor man may be spiritually bound by envy
of another's goods. But action now—as always—must be the proof of this "spiritual
freedom."

Yet it would be an error if we wanted
simply to give away our riches. What is required is the willingness to carry out structural changes at home in the interest of the
Third World, changes that may possibly
touch our own assets. It could mean the im-
position of higher taxes to support effective
foreign aid or the revision of our agricultural
policy in favor of poorer countries or the
opening of our markets for finished products
from the developing countries.

Although no informed person would question the need for such measures, the prob-

ability that they will be enacted is slight in the face of overpowering self-interests. For example, the experts tell us that a number of developing nations, dependent on the export of certain agricultural products, can be helped only if we are ready for encroachments upon our own agriculture. But they emphasize that whoever touches this ticklish matter commits "political suicide."

Will the Christians in our society contribute to the establishment of a climate of public opinion that will make possible the carrying out of necessary but unpopular decisions?

The salvation of Christ is not completed in political liberation, but political liberation finds its place and its true significance in the total liberation incessantly announced by Sacred Scripture . . . . A people of God that promotes the good of every man and of the whole man is what God wills and people wait for. For the Peruvian ecclesial community this implies an option for the oppressed and marginated as a personal and communal commitment. This option does not exclude from our charity any man. To choose those who today experience the most violent forms of oppression is for us an effective way to love also those who, perhaps unconsciously, are oppressed by the very fact that they are oppressors.

Peruvian Catholic Bishops pre-Synod Statement, 1971, nos. 8-9, in *NADOC*, no. 220

It may be that the challenge will be too great. It may be deemed political suicide to speak of problems of development in blunt terms, to force a consideration of unpleasant alternatives and moral dilemmas, to encourage governments whose political and economic structures are alien and even antipathetic to ours. It may appear impractical to urge an internationalization of foreign aid; impolitic to engage in an uncompromising campaign for racial equality; unnecessary to press forward on a hundred difficult fronts of domestic reform. In other words,

the actions which are open to us may be
open only in theory, in the abstract, and not
in hard fact.

Robert L. Heilbroner, economic historian,
in *The Great Ascent,* p. 182

---

i was hungry and . . .

*"When the Son of man comes in his glory,
and all the angels with him, then he will
sit on his glorious throne. Before him
will be gathered all the nations, and he
will separate them one from another as
a shepherd separates the sheep from the
goats, and he will place the sheep at his
right hand, but the goats at the left.
Then the King will say to those at his
right hand, 'Come, O blessed of my Father,
inherit the kingdom prepared for you from
the foundation of the world; for I·was
hungry and you gave me food, I was thirsty
and you gave me drink, I was a stranger
and you welcomed me, I was naked and you
clothed me, I was sick and you visited*

me, I was in prison and you came to me.'
Then the righteous will answer him, 'Lord,
when did we see thee hungry and feed
thee, or thirsty and give thee drink?
And when did we see thee a stranger and
welcome thee, or naked and clothe thee?
And when did we see thee sick or in
prison and visit thee?' And the King will
answer them, 'Truly, I say to you, as you
did it it to one of the least of these my
brethren, you did it to me.' Then he will
say to those at his left hand, 'Depart
from me, you cursed, into the eternal fire
prepared for the devil and his angels; for
I was hungry and you gave me no food, I
was thirsty and you gave me no drink, I
was a stranger and you did not welcome me,
naked and you did not clothe me, sick and
in prison and you did not visit me.'
Then they also will answer, 'Lord, when
did we see thee hungry or thirsty or a
stranger or naked or sick or in prison,
and did not minister to thee?' Then he
will answer them, 'Truly, I say to you,
as you did it not to one of the least of
these, you did it not to me . . . .' "

Matthew 25:31-45

I began to have a bitter taste in my mouth. I thought: is there no end to the bitterness of life? I think that when I was born I was marked by fate to go hungry. I filled one sack of paper. When I entered Paulo Guimarães Street, a woman gave me some newspapers. They were clean and I went to the junk yard picking up everything that I found. Steel, tin, coal, everything serves the *favelado*. Leon weighed the paper and I got six cruzeiros.

I wanted to save the money to buy beans but I couldn't because my stomach was screaming and torturing me.

I decided to do something about it and bought a bread roll. What a surprising effect food has on our organisms. Before I ate, I saw the sky, the trees, and the birds all yellow, but after I ate, everything was normal to my eyes.

Food in the stomach is like fuel in machines. I was able to work better. My body stopped weighing me down. I started to walk faster. I had the feeling that I was gliding in space. I started to smile as if I was witnessing a beautiful play. And will there ever be a drama more beautiful than that of eating? I felt that I was eating for the first time in my life.

Child of the Dark, the Diary of Carolina Maria de Jesus, a Brazilian slum dweller, pp. 52-53

I chose Christianity because I felt that in it I had found the best way of serving my neighbor. I was elected by Christ to be a priest forever, motivated by the desire to devote myself full-time to loving my fellow man.

As a sociologist I wished this love to become effective through science and technique. Upon analyzing Colombian society I realized the need for a revolution that would give food to the hungry, drink to the thirsty, clothing to the naked, and bring about the well-being of the majorities in our country.

I feel that the revolutionary struggle is a Christian and priestly struggle. Only through this, given the concrete circumstances of our country, can we fulfill the love that men should have for their neighbors.

Camilo Torres, Colombian revolutionary and laicized Catholic priest, in *Revolutionary Writings*, p. 163

---

light for the world?

"You are the light of the world. A city set on a hill cannot be hid. Nor do men light a lamp and put it under a bushel, but on a stand, and it gives light to all in the house. Let your light so shine before men, that they may see your good works and give glory to your Father who is in heaven. . . ."   Matthew 5:14-16

Christianity is so identified with the Western powers that many non-Christians, especially in Asia and Africa, regard the Church as a tool of Western imperialism.

Daisuke Kitagawa, Japan, of the Division of World Mission and Evangelism of the World Council of Churches, in *The Maze of Peace*, p. 86

Unless the Church, its members, and its organizations express God's love for man by involvement and leadership in constructive protest against the present conditions of man, then it will become identified with injustice and persecution. If this happens it will die and, humanly speaking, deserves to die because it will then serve no purpose comprehensible to modern man.

Julius K. Nyerere, President of Tanzania, in *Maryknoll* magazine, June 1971, p. 37

An obligation falls on the Church in the United States to seek democratically a reordering of our nation's priorities in a manner that is positive and effective in promoting world justice.

Cardinal John Dearden of Detroit speaking for the Catholic Bishops of the US at the Synod in Rome, October 1971

6. where do
the churches stand?

the new people of god

For in Christ Jesus you are all sons
of God, through faith. For as many of you
as were baptized into Christ have put on
Christ. There is neither Jew nor Greek,
there is neither slave nor free, there is
neither male nor female; for you are all
one in Christ Jesus.   Galatians 3:26-28

All men have become neighbors to one another. Torn by our diversities and tensions,
we do not yet know how to live together.
>Fourth Assembly of the World Council of
>Churches, Uppsala, Sweden, in *Uppsala*
>*Speaks*, p. 5

So the world is not one, its people are more
divided now, and also more conscious of
their divisions, than they have ever been before. They are divided between those who
are satisfied and those who are hungry; they
are divided between those with power and
those without power; they are divided be-

tween those who dominate and those who are dominated, between those who exploit and those who are exploited. And it is the minority which is well fed and the minority which has secured control of the world's wealth and over their fellow men.

Further, in general, that minority is distinguished by the color of their skin, and by their race. And the nations in which most of the minority of the world's people live have a further distinguishing characteristic—their adoption of the Christian religion.

Julius K. Nyerere, President of Tanzania, in *Maryknoll* magazine, June 1971, p. 38

It is, in fact, the goal of the Church to represent that "new people of God" of whom one can say: "There is neither Jew nor Gentile, neither Greek nor barbarian, neither master nor slave, neither man nor woman [and if we may proceed with modern relevance: neither black nor white, neither Communist nor anti-Communist] for all are one in Christ Jesus." The barriers which men erect between each other to assert themselves and humiliate others are demolished in the community of Christ, since men are there affirmed in a new way: they are "children of freedom." By undermining and demolishing all barriers—whether of religion, race, education, or class—the community of Christians proves that it is the community of Christ. This could indeed become the new identifying mark of the Church in our world, that is composed, not of equal and likeminded men, but of dissimilar men, indeed even of former enemies. This would mean, on the other hand, that national churches, class churches, and race churches are false churches of Christ and already heretical as a result of their concrete structure.

Jurgen Moltmann, German theologian, in *Religion, Revolution and the Future*, p. 141

he ends our hostility

*Remember that you were at that time
separated from Christ, alienated from the
commonwealth of Israel, and strangers to
the covenants of promise, having no hope
and without God in the world. But now in
Christ Jesus you who once were far off have
been brought near in the blood of Christ.
For he is our peace, who has made us both
one, and has broken down the dividing
wall of hostility, by abolishing in his
flesh the law of commandments and
ordinances, that he might create in himself
one new man in place of the two, so making
peace, and might reconcile us both to God
in one body through the cross, thereby
bringing the hostility to an end. And he
came and preached peace to you who were
far off and peace to those who were near;
for through him we both have access in one
Spirit to the Father.* Ephesians 2:12-18

World military expenditures, inflated by further increases in prices, reached a new peak in 1970. Last year's world total reached an estimated $204,000,000,000, the equivalent in dollar value of a year's income produced by the 1,800,000,000 people in the poorer half of the world's population.

> US Arms Control and Disarmament Agency in *World Military Expenditures, 1970*, p. 1

Peace is no excuse for the arms race for it cannot be built or maintained by violence or terror . . . . The arms race is indeed a plague to all humanity in both developed and developing nations . . . . Today strategic arsenals are loaded with nuclear power capable of destroying all life with the over-kill equivalent of 15 tons of dynamite for every human person.

> Cardinal John Krol of Philadelphia speaking for the Catholic Bishops of the US at the Synod in Rome, October 1971

The world and mankind are marked by sin and characterized by its consequences of injustice, deprivation, exploitation, and oppression. The unity for which Christ prayed to the Father (John 17:21) is the vocation of the entire world (Col. 1:20; Eph. 1:4-10) and the special task of the Church, which presents itself as a sacrament of the unity of the world. The unity of all men is possible only with effective justice for all.

Peruvian Catholic Bishops pre-Synod Statement,.1971, no. 24, in *NADOC*, no. 220

---

you are one body

For just as the body is one and has many members, and all the members of the body, though many, are one body, so it is with Christ. For by one Spirit we were all baptized into one body—Jews or Greeks, slaves or free—and all were made to drink of one Spirit.

For the body does not consist of one member but of many. If the foot should say, "Because I am not a hand, I do not belong to the body," that would not make

it any less a part of the body. And if the
ear should say, "Because I am not an eye,
I do not belong to the body," that would
not make it any less a part of the body.
If the whole body were an eye, where would
be the hearing? If the whole body were an
ear, where would be the sense of smell?
But as it is, God arranged the organs in
the body, each one of them, as he chose.

If all were a single organ, where would
the body be? As it is, there are many
parts, yet one body. The eye cannot say
to the hand, "I have no need of you,"
nor again the head to the feet, "I have
no need of you." On the contrary, the
parts of the body which seem to be weaker
are indispensable, and those parts of
the body which we think less honorable we
invest with the greater honor, and our
unpresentable parts are treated with
greater modesty, which our most presentable
parts do not require. But God has so
adjusted the body, giving the greater
honor to the inferior part, that there may
be no discord in the body, but that the
members may have the same care for one
another. If one member suffers, all

suffer together; if one member is honored,
all rejoice together.   I Corinthians 12:12-26

The present population of Earth is estimated at 3,500 million people and calculations, based on success of present population control programmes, put it at 6,500 million by the year 2000 .... As many as two-thirds of the world's present population are suffering from malnutrition and the threat of large-scale famine is still with us despite some nutritional advances .... It has been estimated that a child born in the United States today will consume during his lifetime at least twenty times as much as one born in India, and contribute about fifty times as much pollution to the environment.

"Menton Message" of 2,200 environmental scientists, in *The UNESCO Courier*, July 1971, p. 5

Because of the polarization of political options among Latin American Christians and the extreme difficulty of the situation, there are some Christians among the oppressed and persecuted and others among the oppressors and persecutors, some among the tortured and others among the torturers or those who condone torture. Thus there is occurring a grave and radical confrontation between Christians who suffer injustice and exploitation and those who benefit from the established order. Under these conditions life in the Christian community is full of difficulties and conflicts. Participation in the Eucharist, for example, as it is celebrated today, is considered by many to be—for want of the support of an authentic community—an exercise in make-believe.

Gustavo Gutiérrez, Peruvian theologian, in *Theology of Liberation,* p. 8

The Gospel of Jesus Christ is the good news that in Christ God has broken down the walls of division between God and man, and therefore also between man and man.

"Message to the South African People" of the theological commission of the Council of African Churches, in *IDOC-NA,* no. 2, p. 85

he emptied himself

Do nothing from selfishness or conceit, but in humility count others better than yourselves. Let each of you look not only to his own interest, but also to the interests of others. Have this mind among yourselves, which you have in Christ Jesus, who, though he was in the form of God, did not count equality with God a thing to be grasped, but emptied himself, taking the form of a servant, being born in the likeness of men. And being found in human form he humbled himself and became obedient unto death, even death on a cross. Therefore God has highly exalted him and bestowed on him the name which is above every name, that at the name of Jesus every knee should bow, in heaven and on earth and under the earth, and every tongue confess that Jesus Christ is Lord, to the glory of God the Father. Philippians 2:3-11

We must conjure up in our mind's eye what underdevelopment means for the two billion human beings for whom it is not a statistic but a living experience of daily life. Unless we can see the Great Ascent from the vantage point of those who must make the climb, we cannot hope to understand the difficulties of the march.

It is not easy to make this mental jump. But let us attempt it by imagining how a typical American family, living in a small suburban house on an income of six or seven thousand dollars, could be transformed into an equally typical family of the under-developed world.

We begin by invading the house of our imaginary American family to strip it of its furniture. Everything goes: beds, chairs, tables, television sets, lamps. We will leave the family with a few old blankets, a kitchen table, a wooden chair. Along with the bureaus go the clothes. Each member of the family may keep in his "wardrobe" his oldest suit or dress, a shirt or blouse. We will permit a pair of shoes to the head of the family, but none for the wife or children.

We move into the kitchen. The appliances

have already been taken out, so we turn to the cupboards and larder. The box of matches may stay, a small bag of flour, some sugar and salt. A few moldy potatoes, already in the garbage can, must be hastily rescued, for they will provide much of tonight's meal. We will leave a handful of onions, and a dish of dried beans. All the rest we take away: the meat, the fresh vegetables, the canned goods, the crackers, the candy.

Now we have stripped the house: the bathroom has been dismantled, the running water shut off, the electric wires taken out. Next we take away the house. The family move to the toolshed . . . .

Communications must go next. No more newspapers, magazines, books—not that they are missed, since we must take away our family's literacy as well. . . .

Now government services must go. No more postman, no more fireman. There is a school, but it is three miles away and consists of two classrooms. They are not too overcrowded since only half the children in the neighborhood go to school. There are, of course, no hospitals or doctors nearby. The nearest clinic is ten miles away and is tended by a midwife. It can be reached by bicycle, provided that the family has a bicycle, which is unlikely. Or one can go by bus—not always inside, but there is usually room on top.

Finally, money. We will allow our family a cash hoard of five dollars . . . .

Meanwhile the head of our family must earn his keep. As a peasant cultivator with three acres to tend, he may raise the equivalent of $100 to $300 worth of crops a year. If he is a tenant farmer, which is more than likely, a third or so of his crop will go to his landlord, and probably another 10 percent to the local moneylender. . . .

And so we have brought our typical American family down to the very bottom of the human scale. It is, however, a bottom in which we can find, give or take a hundred million souls, at least a billion people.

Robert L. Heilbroner, economic historian, in *The Great Ascent,* pp. 33-37

All our people are sons of God, brothers of equal stature. How can we get this point across while we offer them different religious services depending on the amount of money they pay? What are we to say about the class-conscious cast of our schools? How can a bishop expel a priest or a group of priests without hearing his body of priests and the Christian community in which they work? By the same token, we cannot understand how the Church could join with the municipality of La Paz to construct steeples when the problems of local underdevelopment are so serious. This would be a perfect opportunity to get people thinking about the illegitimacy of building churches with money robbed from the exploited worker. Instead of talking about the Church of the poor, we must be a poor Church. And we flaunt this commitment with our real estate, our rectories and other buildings, and our whole style of life. All of us bear a share of the blame here.

Statement of 80 Bolivian Catholic priests, in *Between Honesty and Hope*, p. 142

dead faith

What does it profit, my brethren, if a man
says he has faith but has not works? Can
this faith save him? If a brother or sister
is ill-clad and in lack of daily food, and
one of you says to them, "Go in peace, be
warmed and filled," without giving them
the things needed for the body, what does
it profit? So faith by itself, if it has
not works, is dead . . . . For as the body
apart from the spirit is dead, so faith
apart from works is dead.   James 2:14-17, 26

The presentation of the Word of God must
be related to the *action* of Christians—or else
we remain mere talkers; and this is the cause
of the present *credibility gap* concerning
Christian interest in man . . . . The exigencies
of the Gospel are very radical and demand-
ing. For example, what is the challenge
placed on us by the story of Dives and
Lazarus in this world of plenty and poverty,
or of the Good Samaritan in the context of

exploitation in Asia? Do we really take Jesus and his Gospel seriously? Many young people and many who are not Christians do not think we do so. If we did we should be at least as dedicated to a meaningful and effective transformation of man and society as are the followers of other less revolutionary and less inspired doctrines such as Marxism.

Episcopal Conference of Ceylon at the Catholic Asian Bishops Meeting, Manila, 1970

To be complacent in the face of the world's need is to be guilty of practical heresy.

Fourth Assembly of the World Council of Churches, Uppsala, Sweden, in *Uppsala Speaks*, p. 51

We call upon the Churches to embrace the liberation struggle in its efforts. The Church has done this in its domestic work. Minority empowerment at home cannot be divorced from the process of de-colonization and nation-building in the Third World. Accordingly, we urge the Church to employ its resources to support the struggle for social

justice now being carried on by oppressed
people throughout the world. We are com-
pelled to call the Churches to a clear, un-
equivocal position of support for relief from
oppression today. This must be done as
surely as the Church supported the abolition
of slavery, the Civil War efforts, and opposi-
tion to Fascism.

Statement of the Interreligious Foundation for Community Organization, a coali-
tion of national religious agencies and
minority community groups, June 1971,
in *IDOC-NA* no. 35, p. 11

---

new life—or dying faith?

*Do you not know that all of us who have
been baptized into Christ Jesus were
baptized into his death? We were buried
therefore with him by baptism into death,
so that as Christ was raised from the
dead by the glory of the Father, we too
might walk in newness of life . . . .*

*Let not sin therefore reign in your
mortal bodies, to make you obey their*

passions. Do not yield your members to sin
as instruments of wickedness, but yield
yourselves to God as men who have been
brought from death to life, and your
members to God as instruments of
righteousness.   Romans 6:3-4, 12-13

How have the Churches in Asia responded to
this revolutionary situation during the past
25 years, i.e., during our lifetime? Without
attempting to pass judgment on individuals,
we may say that the Churches have in large
measure been irrelevant to these changes. We
have generally disregarded socio-economic
analysis and been indifferent to political and
economic exploitation both internal and external. We have been implicitly on the side
of the status quo, at least by our seemingly
approving *silence*. Sometimes we have been
accomplices in the processes of alienation of
the Asian peoples and even benefited from
the presence and power of the exploiters. In
fact we have been on the side of practical
capitalism in a rather uncritical manner,
sometimes perhaps unconsciously helping it,

propagating it, legitimizing it and even tending to consecrate it. Our Churches, priestly and religious life have tended to accept the values of capitalist society and fit themselves within its framework.

Tissa Balasuriya, O.M.I., President of Aquinas University, Ceylon, in *World Parish* (Maryknoll, N.Y.), January 1972

What we have already said and the experience of our people lead to the rejection of capitalism, both in its economic aspects as well as in its ideological foundation which favors individualism, profit, and the exploitation of man by man himself. Thus we must strive to create a qualitatively different society.

Peruvian Catholic Bishops pre-Synod Statement, 1971, no. 10, in *NADOC*, no. 220

is waiting enough?

*According to his promise we wait for new
heavens and a new earth in which
righteousness dwells.* 2 Peter 3:13

All the political goodwill and all the instruments of social and economic development
at the disposal of the rich and poor countries
must be combined and be harnessed with a
new spirit of dedication, sacrifice, wisdom,
and foresight to meet our common obligation to the whole of humanity. This calls for
a new and global vision of man and the
human race . . . . The challenge is not just
simply the elimination of poverty, ignorance, and disease. It is first and foremost a
question of building a world in which every
man, woman, and child, without distinction,
will have and exercise the right to live a full
human life worthy of his or her person, free
from servitude, oppression, and exploitation
imposed on him or her by other fellow hu-

man beings; a world in which freedom, peace, and security will have practical meaning to each and every member of the human race.   Kenneth Kaunda, President of Zambia, at the Fourth Assembly of the World Council of Churches, Uppsala, Sweden

The Church cannot stand apart. Our common manhood under God involves responsible and just stewardship of the world's resources just as much as caring for our neighbor. The vision that beckons the Churches forward in the concern for development is the vision of the one human family, in which all members will have the opportunity to live truly human lives and so as men respond to the purposes of God.

> *Ten Crucial Years,* statement on the Second Development Decade and the Task of the Churches, by the Commission on the Churches' Participation in Development of the World Council of Churches

what is god's will?

Do not be conformed to this world but be transformed by the renewal of your mind, that you may prove what is the will of God, what is good and acceptable and perfect.

Romans 12:2

What horror has the world come to when it uses profit as the prime incentive in human progress and competition as the supreme law of economics!

Dom Helder Camara, Catholic Archbishop of Olinda and Recife, Brazil, at Fordham University, January 1972

At the moment, governments in affluent countries are apt to maintain that, while they realize that they ought to be doing more in this field [of development], for reasons of self-interest as well as altruism, they cannot do so when the man-in-the-street is adopting such a disinterested attitude. From the *Financial Times*, London, quoted in *CERES* (FAO Review), March-April 1971, p. 19

God is concerned in such technical problems as liquidity, the terms of trade, tariffs, and infrastructural development. To think or act otherwise is to create a false dichotomy and to try to confine God within an ecclesiastical system divorced from the world he died to save.   Official Report of the World Conference on Church and Society of the World Council of Churches, Geneva, pp. 89-90

---

love does no wrong

Love does no wrong to a neighbor;
therefore love is the fulfilling of
the law.   Romans 13:10

Each car which Brazil puts on the road denies fifty people good transportation by bus. Each merchandised refrigerator reduces the chance of building a community freezer. Every dollar spent in Latin America on doctors and hospitals costs a hundred lives, to adopt a phrase of Jorge de Ahumada, the brilliant Chilean economist. Had each dollar been spent on providing safe drinking water, a hundred lives could have been saved. Each dollar spent on schooling means more privileges for the few at the cost of the many; at best it increases the number of those who, before dropping out, have been taught that those who stay longer have earned the right to more power, wealth, and prestige.

Ivan Illich, Director of the CIDOC Documentation Center, Cuernavaca, Mexico, in *The New York Review of Books*, November 6, 1969

Reformism and its methods have not brought the bold and vital changes we require. In fact, one would be immoral and iniquitous to favor slow, gradual change, because that would be tantamount to keeping alive the institutionalized oppression we face. Jorge Manrique, Catholic Archbishop of La Paz, Bolivia, in *IDOC-NA*, no. 16, p. 52

how does god's love abide in him?

*We know that we have passed out of death
into life, because we love the brethren.
He who does not love remains in death. Any
one who hates his brother is a murderer,
and you know that no murderer has eternal
life abiding in him. By this we know love,
that he laid down his life for us; and
we ought to lay down our lives for the
brethren. But if anyone has the world's
goods and sees his brother in need, yet
closes his heart against him, how does
God's love abide in him? Little children,
let us not love in word or speech but in
deed and in truth.*   I John 3:14-18

"He who loves fulfills the law," says St.
Paul. "Love and do what you will," says St.
Augustine. The surest sign of predestination
is love of neighbor. St. John tells us: "If
someone says he loves God, whom he does
not see, and does not love his neighbor
whom he does see, he is a liar."

However, this love for our neighbor must be effective. We will not be judged only by our good intentions, but mainly by our actions in favor of Christ represented in each one of our neighbors. "I was hungry and you did not give me to eat, I was thirsty and you did not give me to drink."

Under the present circumstances in Latin America we see that we cannot feed, or clothe, or house the majorities. Those who hold power constitute an economic minority which dominates political, cultural, and military power, and, unfortunately, also ecclesiastical power in the countries in which the Church has temporal goods. This minority will not make decisions opposed to its own interests. For this reason governmental decisions are not made to benefit the majorities. In order to give them food, drink, and clothing, basic decisions are necessary, decisions which can only come from the government. Technical solutions we have or we can obtain. But who decides on their application? The minority, against its own interests? It is a sociological absurdity that a group would act against its own interests. The power must be taken for the majorities' part so that structural, economic, social, and political reforms benefiting these majorities may be realized. This is called revolution, and if it is necessary in order to fulfill love for one's neighbor, then it is necessary for a Christian to be revolutionary.

> Camilo Torres, Colombian revolutionary and laicized Catholic priest, in *Revolutionary Writings*, pp. 167-68

The harsh facts we have yet to acknowledge are these: (1) in many countries of the underdeveloped world only revolutionary activity will rescue the populace from its unending misery, and (2) the United States has consistently opposed the kinds of revolutionary action that might begin such a rescue operation.

> Robert L. Heilbroner, economic historian, in *Harper's Magazine,* September, 1968, p. 65

the harsh reality

Look carefully then how you walk, not as unwise men but as wise, making the most of the time, because the days are evil.

Ephesians 5:15-16

Why should the United States voluntarily give up the power to use aid and trade policies to solve its balance of payments, agricultural surplus, raw materials, and consumer export problems? To do so would require Americans to solve these problems in other ways involving domestic political and economic dislocations. The Administration and the Congress are under strong and continuing pressure from a variety of powerful special political interests to grant concessions to American citizens at the expense of poor countries which have neither lobbies nor votes. Why should the United States encourage exports from poor countries which will put American factories out of business, laborers out of work, and raise prices even more at the supermarket? Why shouldn't the United States continue to use its political leverage to preserve economic advantages?

Richard J. Barnet, Director of the Institute for Policy Studies, in *Can the United States Promote Foreign Development?*, p. 22

In order to participate in the Asian revolution we must courageously articulate an adequate teaching on *international social justice*, as did the prophets of old concerning the society of their day. We must stand unhesitatingly for the liberation of the oppressed, for the removal of the onus of debt of the poor, for the provision of land to the landless, work to the jobless, houses for the shelterless, food for the hungry, freedom for captives, and justice for all. These constitute some of the basic urges of the modern Asian revolution, and these are also the main burden of the Gospel message.

Tissa Balasuriya, O.M.I., President of Aquinas University, Ceylon, in *World Parish* (Maryknoll, N.Y.), January 1972

7. what god
reserves to himself

behold, i make all things new!

Then I saw a new heaven and a new earth;
for the first heaven and the first earth
had passed away, and the sea was no more.
And I saw the holy city, new Jerusalem,
coming down out of heaven from God,
prepared as a bride adorned for her
husband; and I heard a great voice from
the throne saying, "Behold, the dwelling
of God is with men. He will dwell with
them, and they shall be his people, and
God himself will be with them; he will
wipe away every tear from their eyes, and
death shall be no more, neither shall there
be mourning nor crying nor pain any more,
for the former things have passed away."
And he who sat upon the throne said,
"Behold, I make all things new."

Revelation 21:1-5

We live in a new world of exciting prospects.
For the first time in history men can see the
unity of mankind as a reality. For the first
time in history we know that all men could

enjoy the prosperity that has hitherto been enjoyed by a few. The new technological possibilities turn what were dreams into realities. The adventure of cooperation with all men for the development of the earth for all men is open for all of us, and youth at least is aware of its pull. As today we have the means, so we are without the excuse of ignorance about the condition of men throughout the earth. It is one world and the gross inequalities between the peoples of different nations and different continents are as inexcusable as the gross inequalities within nations.

Report of the Beirut Conference on World Development, sponsored by the World Council of Churches and the Pontifical Commission Justice and Peace, p. 16

Our hope is in him who makes all things new. He judges our structures of thought and action and renders them obsolete. If our false security in the old and our fear of revolutionary change tempt us to defend the status quo or to patch it up with half-hearted measures, we may all perish. The death of the old may cause pain to some, but failure to build up a new world community may bring death to all. In their faith in the coming Kingdom of God and in their search for his righteousness, Christians are urged to participate in the struggle of millions of people for greater social justice and for world development.

Fourth Assembly of the World Council of Churches, Uppsala, Sweden, in *Uppsala Speaks*, p. 45

We are especially concerned with the widening gap between the poor of the world and the rich—not only of material goods, as the rich get richer, and the poor remain in misery—but the growing gap in understanding. The indifference of the well-to-do is perhaps the major obstacle in the world today.

We feel we must warn the people of the world that present trends tend toward the permanent pauperization of 2/3 of the people of the world. The poor people of every nation are being locked out of the system of opportunity to remain in misery for future generations, unless mankind can find and choose a better way to live together.

But we two—Baptist Pastor and Catholic Bishop, US and Brazilian citizens—are not discouraged. There is hope, and there is a great dream of a world in which there will be no more misery, no more war, no more prejudice, and all men will be free. This was the dream of Jesus Christ, of Mahatma Gandhi, and of Martin Luther King, Jr. This is our dream, too.

Ralph Abernathy and Dom Helder Camara, *The Declaration of Recife*, March 1970

8. "i was hungry . . ."

". . . I was hungry and you gave me food,
I was thirsty and you gave me drink, I was
a stranger and you welcomed me, I was naked
and you clothed me, I was sick and you
visited me, I was in prison and you came
to me . . . ."   Matthew 25:35-36

---

1. Gross National Product
(US dollars per capita)

Bolivia	$ 177
Ethiopia	63
France	2,536
Haiti	65
India	82
Indonesia	95
Iraq . . . . : . .	278
Tanzania	78
United States	4,304

2. Food Consumption (Calories per day)
(Minimum Daily Requirement: 2,700)

Bolivia	2,060
Ethiopia	2,150
France	3,180
Haiti	1,720
India	1,900
Indonesia	1,870
Iraq	1,920
Tanzania	2,140
United States	3,240

3. Life Expectation at Birth

Bolivia	50
Ethiopia	na
France	75 (f); 68 (m)
Haiti	33
India	41 (f); 42 (m)
Indonesia	47
Iraq	na
Tanzania	41
United States	74 (f); 67 (m)

4. Infant Mortality Rates
(Deaths under 1 year of age per 1,000 live births)

Bolivia	77
Ethiopia	na
France	16
Haiti	na
India	139
Indonesia	87
Iraq	16
Tanzania	160
United States	21

5. Public Health Expenditures
(US dollars per capita)

Bolivia	$ 1
Ethiopia	1
France	6
Haiti	1
India	1
Indonesia	--
Iraq	3
Tanzania	1
United States	106

6. Population Per Physician

Bolivia	2,680
Ethiopia	71,790
France	770
Haiti	13,420
India	4,830
Indonesia	27,560
Iraq	3,830
Tanzania	23,170
United States	650

---

7. Public Education Expenditures
(US dollars per capita)

Bolivia	$ 6
Ethiopia	1
France	67
Haiti	1
India	2
Indonesia	1
Iraq	15
Tanzania	2
United States	231

8. University Level Education
(Students enrolled per 100,000 population)

Bolivia 414
Ethiopia 17
France 1,239
Haiti 34
India 225
Indonesia 175
Iraq 419
Tanzania 9
United States 3,471

---

9. Foreign Economic Aid Given
(US dollars per capita)

Bolivia . . . . $ --
Ethiopia . . . .
France 20
Haiti . . . .
India . . . . --
Indonesia . . . .
Iraq . . . . --
Tanzania . . . . --
United States 20

10. Military Expenditures
(US dollars per capita)

Bolivia	$ 4
Ethiopia	2
France	123
Haiti	1
India	3
Indonesia	3
Iraq	32
Tanzania	4
United States	401

--	None or negligible
na	Data not available
(m)	male
(f)	female

Sources: Most recent statistics cited in the United Nations *Statistical Yearbook, 1970;* the United Nations *Demographic Yearbook, 1969*; the UNESCO *Statistical Yearbook 1969*; and the US Arms Control and Disarmament Agency's *World Military Expenditures, 1970.*

suggestions for further reading

Most of the contemporary quotations used in *the radical bible* are taken from the following. Those marked with an asterisk (*) are especially recommended as introductory reading on the subject of development and social justice.

Barnet, Richard J. *Can the United States Promote Foreign Development?* Overseas Development Council Paper 6. Washington, D.C., 1971.

*Between Honesty and Hope. Documents from and about the Church in Latin America; Issued at Lima by the Peruvian Bishops' Commission for Social Action. Maryknoll, New York: Maryknoll Publications, 1970.

Camara, Helder. *The Church and Colonialism: The Betrayal of the Third World.* Denville, New Jersey: Dimension Books, 1969.

Child of the Dark: The Diary of Carolina Maria de Jesus. New York: E. P. Dutton & Co., Inc., 1962.

Christians in the Technical and Social Revolutions of Our Time. Official Report of the World Conference on Church and Society, Geneva, July 1966. Geneva: World Council of Churches, 1967.

The Church in the Present-Day Transformation of Latin America in the Light of the Council. Documents of the Second General Conference of Latin American Bishops held at Medellín, Colombia, August-September 1968. Vol. 2, *Conclusions.* Bogota: General Secretariat of CELAM, 1970.

The Development Apocalypse (or) Will International Injustice Kill the Ecumenical Movement? Special Issue of *Risk,* quarterly published by the Youth Department of the World Council of Churches and the World Council of Christian Education, vol. 3, no. 1 and 2, 1967.

The Documents of Vatican II. Ed. Walter M. Abbot, S.J. New York: Herder and Herder, Association Press, 1966.

Fahey, Joseph J. *Peace, War and the Christian Conscience.* New York: The Christophers, 1970.

Fenton, Thomas P. *Coffee–The Rules of the Game and You.* New York: The Christophers, 1972.

Gandhi, Mahatma. *All Men Are Brothers.* Paris:

UNESCO and New York: Columbia University Press, 1958.

Goulet, Denis. *The Cruel Choice: A New Concept in the Theory of Development.* New York: Atheneum, 1971.

Goulet, Denis and Hudson, Michael. *The Myth of Aid: The Hidden Agenda of the Development Reports.* New York: IDOC North America and Maryknoll, N.Y.: Orbis Books, 1971.

Gutiérrez, Gustavo. The Theology of Liberation. Maryknoll, New York: Orbis Books, 1972.

Heilbroner, Robert L. *The Great Ascent.* New York: Harper & Row, Publishers, 1963.

IDOC-INTERNATIONAL, North American Edition. "International Documentation on the Contemporary Church." Published 22 times a year. 432 Park Avenue South, New York, N.Y. 10016.

LADOC. Documentation Service of the Latin American Bureau of the United States Catholic Conference. 1401 K Street, N.W., Washington, D.C. 20025

The Maze of Peace: Conflict and Reconciliation Among Nations. Ed. Alan Geyer. New York: Friendship Press, 1969.

Moltmann, Jurgen. *Religion, Revolution, and the Future.* New York: Charles Scribner's Sons, 1969.

* Myrdal, Gunnar. *The Challenge of World Poverty: A World Anti-Poverty Program in Outline.* New York: Pantheon Books, 1970.

NADOC. Latin American Documentation Service on Development, published by Noticias Aliadas, Apdo. 5594, Lima 1, Peru.

The Nations Speak, 1969. Summary of Policy Statements on the World Situation during the General Debate at the Twenty-Fourth Session of the General Assembly of the United Nations. United Nations, New York: Office of Public Information, 1969.

Nyerere, Julius K. *Freedom and Socialism.* Dar es Salaam: Oxford University Press, 1968.

On the Developed and the Developing. Occasional paper published by the Center for the Study of Democratic Institutions, Santa Barbara, California.

Our Claim on the Future: A Controversial Collection from Latin America. Ed. Jorge Lara-Braud. New York: Friendship Press, 1970.

Pope Paul VI. *This Is Progress.* Chicago: Claretian Publishers, 1968.

Scott, John. *Hunger: A Background Book on Man's Struggle to Feed Himself.* New York: Parents' Magazine Press, 1969.

Smith, John Coventry and Baker, Wesley C. *The Word and the Act: A Study for Christians on Development.* Published by the United Presbyterian Church in the U.S.A.

Torres, Camilo. *Revolutionary Writings.* New York: Herder and Herder, 1969.

Uppsala Speaks. Section Reports of the Fourth Assembly of the World Council of Churches, Uppsala, 1968. Geneva: World Council of Churches and New York: Friendship Press, 1968.

Ward, Barbara. *Spaceship Earth.* New York: Columbia University Press, 1966.

World Development: The Challenge to the Churches. Official Report of the Conference on World Cooperation for Development held in Beirut, Lebanon, April 1968, to the World Council of Churches and the Pontifical Commission Justice and Peace. Geneva: Exploratory Committee on Society, Development and Peace, 1968.

suggestions for action

The Bible is not only a book to read; it is also a way of life. If we attempt to live according to the Scriptures, we must realize that we are being called into action. As the selections in *the radical bible* indicate, the perspective of our action should be global. For we know that the implications of our inaction are global.

Most of us can do little by ourselves. Our first step should be to get in touch with others who are already involved in the world struggle for justice. There are hundreds of groups and organizations in the United States which focus on world affairs or international justice. One of these, *Project 4—A Maryknoll Project for Justice and Peace* (110 Walsh Building, Maryknoll, NY) has especially prepared a follow-up study/action packet for readers of *the radical bible.* This *Third World Packet* includes a bibliography of books, films, and periodicals; learning activities for classroom or discussion groups; a listing of resource groups; and background readings on many of the issues raised in *the radical bible*. To obtain a *Third World Packet* send $1 to cover costs of printing and mailing to Project 4.

For a listing and description of over 200 other educational and action groups representing a variety of special concerns and a spectrum of political opinion, write for the special issue of *Intercom* (May-June 1969), entitled "U.S. Voluntary Organizations and World Affairs" ($1.50 from *Intercom,* Center for War/Peace Studies, 218 E. 18th Street, New York, N.Y. 10003). Some examples of the listings:

1. *National Council of the Churches of Christ in the U.S.A., 475* Riverside Dr., New York, N.Y. 10027, *Department of International Affairs:* Serves as a Christian witness concerning the positions of our nation and its government relative to international order, justice, freedom, and peace; undertakes programs of education and action,

research and development, among clergy and laity, including nationwide study and discussion programs on world affairs, international consultations, national conferences, seminar sessions for leaders at the Church Center for the UN; issues materials; audiovisual aids.

2. *United States Catholic Conference, Department of International Affairs, Division of World Justice and Peace*, 1312 Massachusetts Ave., N.W., Washington, D.C. 20005: Stimulates awareness among U.S. Catholics of their responsibility for promotion of world justice, development and peace. Creates a "conscience lobby" for the poor of the world; develops an awareness of and commitment to the urgent needs of the "third world"; recommends dioceses programs and seminars; promotes panel discussions, workshops, and study projects; issues discussion and program materials.

3. *Friends Committee on National Legislation*, 245 Second St., N.E., Washington, D.C. 20002: Quaker lobby group conducts numerous activities designed to influence

legislation, disseminate information and encourage local discussion on issues of peace and human rights; arranges testimony before Congressional committees; interviews legislators; sponsors seminars; issues materials.

4. *Overseas Development Council*, 1717 Massachusetts Ave., N.W., Washington, D.C. 20036: Keeps tab on research being done on development including trade and foreign investment; determines additional needs and encourages and supports their fulfillment; disseminates information through publications, conferences, seminars, and liaison with other national organizations.

5. *American Freedom from Hunger Foundation*, 1717 H St., N.W., Rm. 437, Washington, D.C. 20006: Seeks to acquaint the American public with the problem of world hunger and the necessity for sending technical assistance to underdeveloped countries as part of worldwide Freedom from Hunger campaign; . . . sponsors community youth mobilization program, "Walks for Development."

acknowledgments

Acknowledgment is gratefully extended to the following for permission to reprint from their works:

E.P. Dutton & Co., Inc.: From *Child of the Dark: The Diary of Carolina Maria de Jesus*. Trans. by David St. Clair. Copyright © 1962 by E.P. Dutton & Co., Inc., and Souvenir Press, Ltd.

Harper & Row, Publishers, Inc.: From *The Great Ascent,* by Robert L. Heilbroner. Copyright © 1963 by Robert L. Heilbroner.

Herder and Herder: From *Revolutionary Writings* by Camilo Torres. Copyright © 1969 by Herder and Herder, Inc.

Overseas Development Council: From *Can the United States Promote Foreign Development?* by Richard J. Barnet. Copyright © 1971 by Overseas Development Council.

World Council of Churches: From *The Development Apocalypse*, a *Risk* paperback, 1967.

All Scriptural quotations are taken from the Revised Standard Version, Old Testament Copyright 1952 and New Testament Copyright 1946 by the Division of Christian Education of the National Council of the Churches of Christ in the United States of America and used with their permission.